Microsoft Dynamics CRM 2011 Customization & Configuration (MB2-866) Certification Guide

A practical guide to customizing and configuring Microsoft Dynamics CRM 2011 focused on helping you pass the certification exam

Neil Benson

PUBLISHING

BIRMINGHAM - MUMBAI

Microsoft Dynamics CRM 2011 Customization & Configuration (MB2-866) Certification Guide

First published: November 2012

Production Reference: 1141112

Published by Packt Publishing Ltd.
Livery Place
35 Livery Street
Birmingham B3 2PB, UK.

ISBN 978-1-84968-580-1

www.packtpub.com

Cover Image by Artie Ng (artherng@yahoo.com.au)

Credits

Author

Neil Benson

Reviewers

Michael Ferreira

Joel Lindstrom

Tanguy Touzard

Jerry Weinstock

Acquisition Editor

Kerry George

Lead Technical Editor

Dayan Hyames

Technical Editor

Prasad Dalvi

Project Coordinator

Joel Goveya

Proofreader

Mario Cecere

Indexer

Tejal Soni

Graphics

Valentina Dsilva

Aditi Gajjar

Production Coordinators

Manu Joseph

Conidon Miranda

Cover Work

Manu Joseph

About the Author

Neil Benson started his CRM career as a sales professional dissatisfied with his organization's CRM system 15 years ago. Since then he has been selling, implementing, and customizing CRM systems with an emphasis on user adoption to maximize return-on-investment. In 2006, he founded Increase CRM, the UK's leading provider of hosted Microsoft Dynamics CRM and he currently works for Slalom Consulting in Los Angeles, California, as a CRM architect. He is a Microsoft Certified Technical Specialist for Microsoft Dynamics CRM and has been a Microsoft Most Valuable Professional for CRM since 2010. He is also a speaker at numerous CRM user groups and Microsoft conferences.

About the Reviewers

Michael Ferreira is a diverse hands-on leader, entrepreneur, and executive consultant with 20 years of widely diverse business and technology leadership experience. He has crafted client/vendor/partner relationships, advisory services, managed large project portfolios, directed product development, implemented transformation change and pioneered new service delivery techniques.

Since 2003 (Microsoft Dynamics CRM 1.0 beta), Michael has been working with a diverse range of customers and partner organizations (start-up to enterprise, across industries). He has proposed, led, architected, and deployed over 100 plus Microsoft CRM-based technology solutions ranging from out-of-the-box configurations to product upgrades to very complex integrated multi-channel service delivery platforms (CRM, ERP, Portal, Mobile, Social, BI/DW with integration).

Beyond implementation, Michael has played a key role in building the Microsoft CRM partner and consultant community having helped launch seven organizational practices/delivery teams as well as in building and selling his own uniquely positioned Microsoft-based technology solutions provider offering professional and managed services, vertical software/platform as a service product, and hardware and software sales.

I'd like to thank Neil and Packt Publishing for letting me participate and my wife for her support throughout the process.

Joel Lindstrom is a CRM consultant based in Greenville, SC. He has been awarded the Microsoft MVP award for the past five years. Prior to working as a CRM consultant, Joel has spent a decade in sales, using a variety of CRM platforms. This experience gave him an appreciation for how the design and configuration choices made in CRM implementation can impact user adoption of the system, either positively or negatively. Joel has helped many clients with CRM installation, deployment, configuration, reporting, and business intelligence, and he is a Scribe MVP. Joel is editor and frequent contributor to the *Customer Effective* blog, the CRM forums, and he has contributed to several CRM books.

Joel works for Customer Effective in Greenville, SC.

> I would like to thank Customer Effective for helping me to grow and be successful, and my wife Stephanie—she inspires me.

Tanguy Touzard is a technical and functional consultant on the Dynamics CRM solution.

He has been working on this solution since 2004, when he became an intern at Microsoft France.

Since then, Tanguy has covered all the technical and functional aspects of the solution—Customizations, Developments, Reporting, Functional, and Consulting.

He currently works for JAVISTA, a French IT company dedicated to Dynamics CRM projects.

Jerry Weinstock has been a long time enthusiast of using technology to enhance sales and marketing practices. Since 1999, he has been providing consulting services in the area of Customer Relationship Management Software, permission-based e-mail marketing, and business process implementation.

In 2010, Microsoft recognized him for his exceptional contributions to the Dynamics CRM technical and business communities when he was awarded the Microsoft Most Valuable Professional status. As a CRM MVP for the last two years, he is a frequent contributor to the *CRM Community Support Forums*.

Jerry is one of the co-authors of *The CRM Field Guide – How to CRM like an MVP with Dynamics CRM*. He also has been a technical reviewer for several other CRM books. Most recent is *Building Business with CRM*.

Jerry is the founder and president of CRM Innovation, Lenexa, Kansas, a Dynamics CRM partner and ISV that provides consulting and implementation services along with building solutions that enhance the sales and marketing automation functionality of Dynamics CRM.

www.PacktPub.com

Support files, eBooks, discount offers and more

You might want to visit www.PacktPub.com for support files and downloads related to your book.

Did you know that Packt offers eBook versions of every book published, with PDF and ePub files available? You can upgrade to the eBook version at www.PacktPub.com and as a print book customer, you are entitled to a discount on the eBook copy. Get in touch with us at service@packtpub.com for more details.

At www.PacktPub.com, you can also read a collection of free technical articles, sign up for a range of free newsletters and receive exclusive discounts and offers on Packt books and eBooks.

http://PacktLib.PacktPub.com

Do you need instant solutions to your IT questions? PacktLib is Packt's online digital book library. Here, you can access, read and search across Packt's entire library of books.

Why Subscribe?

- Fully searchable across every book published by Packt
- Copy and paste, print and bookmark content
- On demand and accessible via web browser

Free Access for Packt account holders

If you have an account with Packt at www.PacktPub.com, you can use this to access PacktLib today and view nine entirely free books. Simply use your login credentials for immediate access.

Instant Updates on New Packt Books

Get notified! Find out when new books are published by following @PacktEnterprise on Twitter, or the *Packt Enterprise* Facebook page.

Dedicated to my wife, Natascha, and to our son, Xander Jenson, who was born while this book was being edited and who taught me to type with one hand.

Table of Contents

Preface

Microsoft Dynamics CRM 2011 Customization and Configuration (MB2-866) Certification Guide will help you prepare for the MB2-866 Microsoft Dynamics CRM 2011 Configuration and Customization certification exam.

This book covers the published exam syllabus as closely as possible to help you prepare for the type of questions that are likely to appear in your exam. Microsoft has published the exam syllabus at `http://www.microsoft.com/learning/en/us/exam.aspx?ID=MB2-866#tab2`.

This book is not a discussion of configuration options or customization best practices. It is written to cover just the material that you need to know to pass the exam.

The book includes the *Test Your Knowledge* sections at the end of each chapter. This section has been designed to check your understanding of the preceding material.

At the end of the book, there is a 75-question sample exam, which mimics the type and style of questions that you will face in the MB2-866 exam. The sample exam questions are not taken from the real exam. This book will help you acquire the knowledge that you need to pass the exam, but it is not an exam dump or cheat guide. If you understand the material covered in this book and practice the procedures covered here, you will pass the exam.

What this book covers

Chapter 1, Microsoft Dynamics CRM 2011 Overview, provides an introduction to the customization architecture of Microsoft Dynamics CRM 2011. It also covers general principles such as supported and unsupported customizations, deployment options, using an implementation methodology, and use of customization security roles.

Chapter 2, Configuring the System Settings, covers the system settings, CRM for Outlook settings, and exportable settings.

Chapter 3, Configuring the Organization Structure, delivers the knowledge necessary to manage business units, users, teams, and security roles to meet an organization's security requirements.

Chapter 4, Entity Customization, shows you how to create custom entities and fields, configure field-level security, use global option sets, manage entities in a solution, and publish customizations.

Chapter 5, Data Modeling Using Entity Relationships, explains relationships and mapping between entities covering the different types of supported relationships, how to configure the entity mappings and connections features.

Chapter 6, User Interface Customization: Forms, Views, and Charts, provides in-depth information on customizing forms, views, and charts including main and mobile forms, using form components, using role-based forms, configuring views, and using system charts.

Chapter 7, Auditing, describes how to configure and use the auditing features of Microsoft Dynamics CRM 2011.

Chapter 8, Solutions, provides the knowledge needed to answer exam questions on creating, exporting, importing, updating, and deleting managed and unmanaged solution packages, and how to work with the managed properties of managed solutions.

Chapter 9, Sample Certification Exam Questions, poses 75 questions similar to those you can expect to find in the MB2-866 exam.

Appendix A, Answers to Sample Certification Exam Questions, provides answers and short explanations to the questions posed in *Chapter 9, Sample Certification Exam Questions*. Remember to try the questions before reading the answers!

Appendix B, Answers to Self-test Questions, provides answers to the questions posed in the *Test your knowledge* section at the end of each chapter.

Appendix C, Introduction to Microsoft Dynamics CRM Training and Certification, discusses the Microsoft Dynamics CRM training courses and certifications. The first half of this chapter will provide a useful overview of the official courses, exams, and certifications that are available. In the second half of the chapter, we'll learn how to book for the MB2-866 exam, what to expect, how to make best use of your time, and how to answer the exam questions.

What you need for this book

You will need a user account with a System Administrator security role for a Microsoft Dynamics CRM 2011 system so that you can practice the configuration and customization procedures outlined in this certification guide.

You can use a Microsoft Dynamics CRM Online 30-day trial system for this purpose. Visit `http://crm.dynamics.com` and follow up the links to sign up for a free 30-day trial.

Alternatively, you can provision an on-premise deployment. For this you will need the following software:

- Microsoft Windows Server 2008 (x64 version) or later, running Active Directory and Internet Information Services 7.0 or later
- Microsoft SQL Server 2008 (x64 version) or later
- Microsoft Dynamics CRM 2011 Server
- Microsoft Dynamics CRM 2011 for Outlook
- Microsoft Outlook 2003 or later, for the CRM for Outlook client

Microsoft provides time-limited evaluation versions of all the required software. Please refer to the *Microsoft Dynamics CRM 2011 Implementation Guide* for further information (`http://www.microsoft.com/en-us/download/details.aspx?id=3621`).

Since the MB2-866 exam was published, Microsoft has released several new features for Microsoft Dynamics CRM 2011. These features are now standard features of the product, but were not available when the exam was published. Throughout the book, you'll find tips about new features that are not examined.

Who this book is for

This book is for anyone who wants to achieve the Microsoft Certified Technology Specialist certification by passing the MB2-866 Microsoft Dynamics CRM 2011 Customization and Configuration exam.

Whether you work for yourself as an independent consultant, work for a Microsoft customer, or work for a Microsoft partner, earning a Microsoft Dynamics CRM certification leads the way to better career opportunities.

Achieving certification demonstrates technical proficiency that validates your knowledge, adds credibility to your resume, and will help you advance in your career. When combined with real-world experience, certification will mean you are more highly regarded than other individuals with similar experience who haven't taken training or shown sufficient initiative to achieve certification.

The topics covered in this book and the exam are intended for anyone implementing or managing Microsoft Dynamics CRM 2011 by using the built-in customization and configuration features.

It also serves as a useful starting point for developers who want to learn about the standard customization features before going on to learn about the development features used to extend Microsoft Dynamics CRM 2011.

It is strongly recommended, but not essential, that readers are familiar with the standard marketing, sales, and service features of Microsoft Dynamics CRM 2011.

Conventions

In this book, you will find a number of styles of text that distinguish between different kinds of information. Here are some examples of these styles, and an explanation of their meaning.

Code words in text are shown as follows: "Form scripting using the documented objects and methods is available by using the `Xrm.Page.data` and `Xrm.Page.ui` objects."

New terms and **important words** are shown in bold. Words that you see on the screen, in menus or dialog boxes for example, appear in the text like this: "In the navigation pane, click on **Settings**."

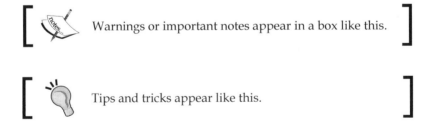

Warnings or important notes appear in a box like this.

Tips and tricks appear like this.

Reader feedback

Feedback from our readers is always welcome. Let us know what you think about this book—what you liked or may have disliked. Reader feedback is important for us to develop titles that you really get the most out of.

To send us general feedback, simply send an e-mail to feedback@packtpub.com, and mention the book title via the subject of your message.

If there is a book that you need and would like to see us publish, please send us a note in the **SUGGEST A TITLE** form on www.packtpub.com or e-mail suggest@packtpub.com.

If there is a topic that you have expertise in and you are interested in either writing or contributing to a book, see our author guide on www.packtpub.com/authors.

Customer support

Now that you are the proud owner of a Packt book, we have a number of things to help you to get the most from your purchase.

Downloading the example code

You can download the example code files for all Packt books you have purchased from your account at http://www.PacktPub.com. If you purchased this book elsewhere, you can visit http://www.PacktPub.com/support and register to have the files e-mailed directly to you.

Errata

Although we have taken every care to ensure the accuracy of our content, mistakes do happen. If you find a mistake in one of our books—maybe a mistake in the text or the code—we would be grateful if you would report this to us. By doing so, you can save other readers from frustration and help us improve subsequent versions of this book. If you find any errata, please report them by visiting http://www.packtpub.com/support, selecting your book, clicking on the **errata submission form** link, and entering the details of your errata. Once your errata are verified, your submission will be accepted and the errata will be uploaded on our website, or added to any list of existing errata, under the Errata section of that title. Any existing errata can be viewed by selecting your title from http://www.packtpub.com/support.

Piracy

Piracy of copyright material on the Internet is an ongoing problem across all media. At Packt, we take the protection of our copyright and licenses very seriously. If you come across any illegal copies of our works, in any form, on the Internet, please provide us with the location address or website name immediately so that we can pursue a remedy.

Please contact us at copyright@packtpub.com with a link to the suspected pirated material.

We appreciate your help in protecting our authors, and our ability to bring you valuable content.

Questions

You can contact us at questions@packtpub.com if you are having a problem with any aspect of the book, and we will do our best to address it.

1
Overview of Microsoft Dynamics CRM 2011

Microsoft Dynamics CRM 2011 provides a range of customization capabilities. This chapter provides an introduction to the CRM application architecture before we learn the different customization capabilities in depth, in later chapters.

We'll discuss the different application tiers and how they can be customized to meet the particular needs of your business. We'll also cover some general principles such as supported and unsupported customizations, differences between deployment options, the benefits of using a repeatable implementation methodology, and the security roles required for customization.

In this chapter we will discuss:

- Architecture of Microsoft Dynamics CRM 2011
- Support and unsupported customizations
- Deployment options
- Using an implementation methodology
- Customization security roles

Architecture of Microsoft Dynamics CRM 2011

Microsoft Dynamics CRM 2011 offers a rich set of marketing, sales, and service features for managing customers. It also offers a rich set of extensibility features for configuring and customizing the standard features, or creating custom features, to meet your requirements.

Multi-tier architecture

Previous generations of business software often had a two-tier, client-server architecture with most of the application logic contained in a rich client that had to be installed on the user's computer while the database was installed on a server.

Microsoft Dynamics CRM is a web-based application that uses a multi-tier client-server architecture. This architecture provides greater scalability, flexibility, and extensibility than a two-tier, client-server architecture. In the multi-tier architecture, the CRM application tier separates the presentation tier from the data tier. The computing resources in the application and data tiers can be increased or decreased depending upon the performance requirements and workload.

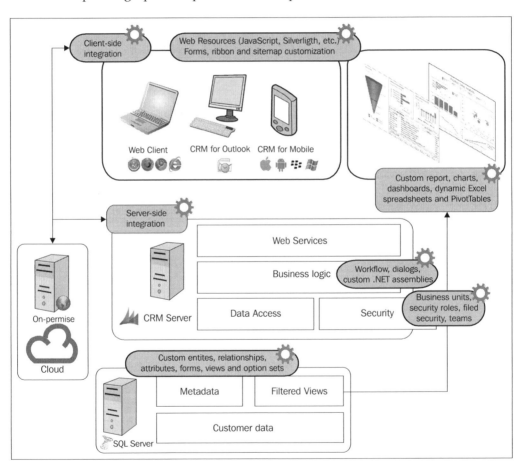

Presentation tier

Microsoft Dynamics CRM 2011 provides user access through the CRM web client, Microsoft Dynamics CRM 2011 for Outlook or Microsoft Dynamics CRM Mobile Express. The presentation tier can be customized using:

- The **user interface customization** features native to Microsoft Dynamics CRM 2011 such as the ability to customize forms and views.

- **Client-side integration with on-premise or cloud-based systems**.

  Using web resources, such as JavaScript and Silverlight, enables rich user-interface customization, data validation, and other client-side features. For example, a Bing Maps integration where a customer address is passed to the Bing Maps service and a map displaying the customer's location is displayed in CRM.

- **Custom reports** by using SQL Server Reporting Services.

- **Custom charts and dashboards** by using the CRM's customization features.

Application tier

The Microsoft Dynamics CRM server runs the application tier (also known as the CRM platform tier) components.

The application tier can be customized by using:

- **Server-side integration** by using the CRM Web services to integrate with on-premise or cloud-based systems.

  For example, when an enquiry form is submitted from a website, a lead is created in the CRM system.

- **Workflows and dialogs** can be configured, using the CRM's customization features. This enables you to automate business processes in the application tier. Processes are triggered by events when specified actions are performed or conditions are met.

  For example, when a sales opportunity's stage is updated to Negotiating, the probability is updated to 90 percent and a notification e-mail is sent to the commercial manager.

- **Plugins and custom workflow activities** can be developed as .NET assemblies in Visual Studio to provide event-based customization.

  For example, when an account's address changes in CRM, the addresses of all the contacts associated with the account are updated. Custom .NET development is outside the scope of the MB2-866 exam.

- **Security** can be customized by creating business units, security roles, field-security profiles, and teams.

Every application that interacts with CRM does so through the web services in the CRM application tier.

Data tier

Microsoft SQL Server provides the data tier components of a Microsoft Dynamics CRM deployment.

The data tier can be customized by using the metadata changes such as creating custom entities, relationships, attributes, forms, views, and option sets. Metadata changes can be made by using the CRM's customization features, importing a solution, or programmatically using the web services. Direct interaction with the data tier—for example, using a SQL statement to create or update records in the CRM database—is not supported.

Filtered views provide an efficient method for securely retrieving the CRM records, using custom SQL-based queries and displaying the data to a user based on their Microsoft Dynamics CRM security roles.

Supported and unsupported customization

Microsoft Dynamics CRM 2011 can be customized by using all the configuration and customization features available in the web client (and described in this guide), and can be extended by using all the methods described in the Microsoft Dynamics CRM **software development kit (SDK)**.

Customizations made by using other methods are unsupported. Unsupported customizations might work initially, but they might not work after updates are applied or the application is upgraded, and these customizations are not supported by Microsoft.

This section describes the most common supported and unsupported customization methods likely to be examined in the MB2-866 exam. For a complete list of supported and unsupported customizations, please refer to the CRM SDK available at http:// msdn.microsoft.com/en-us/library/gg328350.aspx.

Supported customizations

In addition to the configuration and customization features available in the web client, the following customizations are also supported (using the CRM SDK):

- Use of the web services including `DiscoveryService`, `OrganizationService`, Organization Data Service, SOAP endpoint for web services, and `DeploymentService`.

- Form scripting using the documented objects and methods is available by using the `Xrm.Page.data` and `Xrm.Page.ui` objects.

- Ribbon customization using `RibbonDiffXML` to add, remove, or hide ribbon elements.

- The solution files can be customized by exporting and extracting the `customization.xml` file, and making modifications to the `Customizations.xml` file as long as the file still conforms to the `CustomizationsSolution.xsd` schema. Ribbon customization, SiteMap customization, form and dashboard customization using FormXML, and saved query customization, all require this technique.

- Plugins to handle custom business logic that are developed using the mechanism described in the CRM SDK are supported and upgradeable. Adding the plugins and custom workflow activities to the `%installdir%\server\bin\` folder is not supported for Microsoft Dynamics CRM Online.

- The custom workflow activities (assemblies) that are developed by using the mechanism described in the CRM SDK and called from the workflow processes, and the ability to edit the XAML workflows, is supported and upgradeable.

- Adding the custom web pages to the `<serverroot>\ISV\<ISV name>` folder is supported, but deprecated. This means this method will work for earlier versions of Microsoft Dynamics CRM that have been upgraded, but it is not supported for new deployments.

Unsupported customizations

The following types of customization are not supported:

- Modifications or additions to the files in the www root directories of Microsoft Dynamics CRM.

- Modifications to the Microsoft Dynamics CRM website, including the filesystem access control lists.

- Use of client certificates.

- Modifications to the physical schema of the CRM databases—such as adding or modifying tables, stored procedures or views, and so on—other than adding or updating database indexes.

- Creating or updating the records directly in the database by using T-SQL or any other method that is not described in the CRM SDK.

- Editing the `Customizations.xml` file within a solution to edit any solution components other than ribbons, forms, SiteMap, or saved queries.

Deployment options

There are three deployment options for Microsoft Dynamics CRM 2011:

- On-premise
- Partner-hosted
- Online

This section summarizes the differences between the deployment options that are relevant to customization and configuration.

On-premise deployment

In an on-premise deployment, the Microsoft customer deploys Microsoft Dynamics CRM in its own data center. In an on-premise deployment, an **internet-facing deployment (IFD)** configuration is optional and only necessary when users outside the customer's network need access to the CRM application.

Partner-hosted deployment

In a partner-hosted deployment, a Microsoft hosting partner deploys Microsoft Dynamics CRM in the partner's data center. Customer access to the CRM application is usually achieved by using an IFD configuration.

Online deployment

In an online deployment, the customer subscribes to the Microsoft Dynamics CRM Online service that is hosted by Microsoft in its data centers.

Deployment differences

There are some important differences between the customization and configuration options available in an on-premise deployment and an online deployment, as described in the following table:

Customization and configuration option	On-premise	Online
Internet Lead Capture feature	Not available	Included
Scheduled reports feature	Included	Not available
Query language for custom reports	SQL or FetchXML	FetchXML only
Maximum number of the custom entities	Unlimited	300
Maximum number of the workflow processes	Unlimited	200
Custom workflow activities (assemblies)	Supported	Not supported
Custom database indexes	Supported	Not supported
Database backup	As required	Upon request
Database restore	As required	Not available

The customization and configuration options of a partner-hosted deployment can vary widely, depending on the service provided by the partner, and are not discussed further here.

Using an implementation methodology

When implementing Microsoft Dynamics CRM 2011, the use of an implementation methodology is highly recommended. An implementation methodology ensures that a proven, repeatable process is followed so that nothing gets overlooked or omitted. The result is a higher-quality system that better matches the requirements of your organization.

Without following a proven methodology, the CRM system gets implemented in an improvised fashion without a clear plan, specification, or design. This often leads to delays, missed requirements, poor user satisfaction, and more expensive implementation costs.

Microsoft Dynamics Sure Step

Microsoft Dynamics Sure Step is a popular implementation methodology released by Microsoft, based on the best practices used by Microsoft Consulting Services and several of Microsoft's partners.

Sure Step provides a range of tools to help Microsoft partners envision, deploy, upgrade, and optimize the Microsoft Dynamics line of business solutions.

Sure Step can be used for the CRM 2011 and CRM Online projects, and tailored to various project types such as the rapid, standard, enterprise, agile, and upgrade projects.

Sure Step is available to Microsoft partners through the PartnerSource website (http://go.microsoft.com/fwlink/?linkid=88066).

Customization security roles

There are two security roles that are often assigned to users who are responsible for customizing CRM:

- **System Administrator**: Users with the System Administrator security role have full access to all the customization features and there are some solution components, such as plugins and web resources, which can be modified, imported, or exported only by a system administrator.

  Users with the System Administrator security role always have all privileges for all system and custom entities.

  The System Administrator security role cannot be modified, and at least one user must have the System Administrator security role assigned to him/her.

- **System Customizer**: Users with the System Customizer security role can customize most of the CRM solution components, with a few restrictions such as plugins and web resources. For this reason, it is more common for developers to be assigned the System Administrator security role within a CRM development environment.

  The System Customizer security role is useful in smaller deployments when it is assigned to a technical super-user who needs to make simple customization changes to the system. For example, the System Customizer role could be assigned to a marketing manager who needs to add fields, modify views, and create system charts and dashboards.

Summary

Microsoft Dynamics CRM 2011 has a multi-tier architecture that provides greater scalability, flexibility, and extensibility than a two-tier, client-server architecture.

The presentation tier displays the user interface through the CRM web client, CRM for Outlook, or CRM for the Mobile clients, and can be customized by using the client-side integration and web resources.

The application tier runs on the CRM server and includes the web servers, business logic, security, and data access components. It can be customized by using the server-side integration, workflows and dialogs, and the plugins and custom workflow activities.

The data tier stores the customer data and metadata. Customization is supported through metadata changes, but direct database access is not supported. Every application that interacts with CRM does so through the web services in the CRM platform. Alternatively, applications can use the SQL-based queries to retrieve the CRM data by using filtered views.

There are a range of supported and unsupported configuration and customization methods available for Microsoft Dynamics CRM 2011. The unsupported methods may work initially, but might not work after an update or upgrade and will not be supported by Microsoft.

Microsoft Dynamics CRM offers the on-premise, partner-hosted, and online deployment options, with a few customization and configuration differences between these options.

Using an implementation methodology, such as Microsoft Dynamics Sure Step, ensures that a proven, repeatable process is followed so that nothing gets overlooked or omitted.

A System Administrator or System Customizer security role is required to customize Microsoft Dynamics CRM 2011. The System Customizer security role has some limitations, such as creating plugins and web resources.

In the next chapter, we'll learn more on how to configure the CRM 2011 system settings.

2
Configuring the System Settings

Microsoft Dynamics CRM 2011 provides a wide range of system settings that can be customized to meet your business requirements. We'll also learn which of the system settings can be included when we export a solution:

In this chapter we will cover:

- Configuring the system settings
- CRM for Outlook settings
- Exportable settings

Configuring the system settings

System settings are configurable settings that apply to the entire system. In this section, we will learn how to configure the system settings for Microsoft Dynamics CRM.

All users experience the same system settings, although some system settings can be superseded by a user's personal options. For example, as the system administrator you can configure the minimum time between synchronizations of CRM for Outlook that applies to all users, but a user can choose to specify a greater time than the minimum time that you have set.

The system settings are arranged into ten groups:

- General
- Calendar
- Formats

- Auditing
- E-mail
- Marketing
- Customization
- Outlook
- Reporting
- Goals

When you export a solution, you can include some of these system settings in your solution. Refer to the *Exportable settings* section, discussed later in this chapter, for more information on settings that can be exported in a solution.

How to configure the system settings

This section describes how to configure the system settings.

Follow these steps to access the **System Settings** pop-up window:

1. In the navigation pane, click on **Settings**.
2. Click on **Administration** and then select **System Settings** in the **Administration** area.

General

To configure the general system settings, perform the following steps:

1. Click on the **General** tab.
2. Specify the following options:
    - **Select the display option for Get Started panes**: The **Get Started** panes that appear in grid screens, such as **Accounts** and **Contacts**, can be useful just after the system is initially released, but you can hide them later by using this option.
    - **Set the IM presence option**: Select whether instant messaging will be enabled or not. When enabled, a presence status indicator will appear beside names of users, contacts, and leads, and users can communicate with the user, contact, or lead by using their instant messaging client such as Windows Messenger or Microsoft Lync.
    - **Set the full-name format**: Select the name format used for user and contact full names. Once changed, the new name format will only apply to new records created after the option has been changed.

- ○ **Set the currency precision that is used for pricing throughout the system**: Select the default number of decimal points used in the currency fields. The currency fields can share this **Pricing Decimal Precision** value throughout the system, or they can share a currency precision depending on the currency, or you can specify a custom precision for each currency field.

- ○ **Set whether reassigned records are shared with the original owner**: The sharing feature can be used to create an exception to the standard organization structure. Imagine an organization with two business units and security roles that prevent a user in one business unit from viewing records in the other business unit. If this option is enabled, the record will be shared with the original owner if the record was reassigned to a new owner in the other business unit, otherwise the original owner will not be able to view the record after it is reassigned.

- ○ **Set blocked file extensions for attachments**: Specify the filename extensions that will be blocked if users try to upload files. This applies to the file attachment feature and the e-mail tracking feature.

- ○ **Set the currency display option**: Specify whether the currency symbol or currency code is used.

3. Click on **OK** to save your changes.

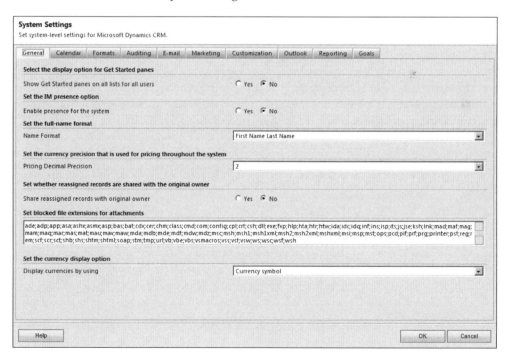

Calendar

To configure the calendar system settings, perform the following steps:

1. Click on the **Calendar** tab.

2. Specify the following options:

   ° **Maximum duration of an appointment in days**

   ° **Maximum number of days for an appointment**

   Users will receive a warning message if they attempt to save an appointment with a duration greater than the one specified in this setting.

3. Click on **OK** to save your changes.

Formats

The formats system setting determines how Microsoft Dynamics CRM displays numbers, currencies, times, and dates.

To configure the formats system settings, perform the following steps:

1. Click on the **Formats** tab.

2. Select a current format to apply the commonly-used settings from a locale, or click on **Customize** and specify the number, currency, time, and date format settings to meet your requirements.

3. Click on **OK** to save your changes.

Changing the format in the **System Settings** area does not change the formats used by the existing users—changes only apply to new user accounts created subsequently. Users can change their own display form in the **Personal Options** area.

Auditing

Organization-level auditing can be enabled in the **System Settings** area.

For detailed information on configuring auditing, please refer to *Chapter 7, Auditing*.

E-mail

To configure the e-mail tracking system settings, follow these steps:

1. Click on the **E-mail** tab.

2. Specify the following options:

    - **Configure e-mail processing**: Specify whether or not the CRM E-mail Router will process e-mail messages only from approved addresses. Each time a new user is created or a user's e-mail address is modified, you will need to approve the user's e-mail address by using the **Approve E-mail** feature on the **Users** grid or the **User** form.

    - **Configure e-mail correlation**: Specify how CRM will correlate replies to the original e-mail message. Tracking token uses a configurable unique string appended to the subject line of e-mail messages. Smart matching uses patterns in the sender, recipients, and subject line.

    - **Set tracking options for e-mails between CRM users**: Specify whether tracked e-mail messages between users will be tracked as one or two e-mail activity records.

    - **Set E-mail form options**: Specify whether or not secure frames will be used to restrict e-mail message content, which means that some HTML content in tracked e-mail messages will not be displayed. Specify whether or not messages with unresolved e-mail addresses can be sent, which will restrict users from sending an e-mail message unless the recipient matches an existing user, lead, contact, or account.

    - **Set file size limit for attachments**: Files attached to an e-mail message will be stored in the CRM database. You can use this option to set the maximum file size in order to prevent large files from consuming the database storage space.

3. Click on **OK** to save your changes.

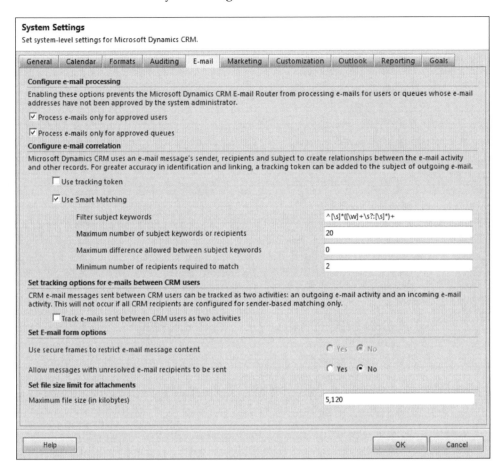

Marketing

To configure the marketing system settings, perform the following steps:

1. Click on the **Marketing** tab.

2. Specify the following options:

    ◦ **Set whether direct e-mail through mail merge is enabled in campaigns**: If this option is enabled, the **Direct E-mail via Mail Merge** feature enables users to deliver e-mail messages based on a Microsoft Word e-mail template using CRM for Outlook through a marketing campaign activity.

- Set whether campaign responses are created for incoming campaign activity e-mail (Available only if E-mail tracking is enabled): Specify whether or not CRM will automatically create a campaign response record, if an inbound e-mail is received in response to an outbound marketing e-mail message.

- Set the auto-unsubscribe options (Available only if E-mail tracking is enabled): Specify how you want to handle requests from customers to unsubscribe from future e-mail marketing campaigns.

3. Click on **OK** to save your changes.

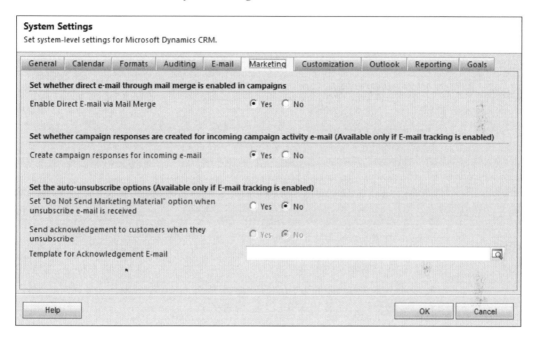

Customization

To configure the customization system settings, follow these steps:

1. Click on the **Customization** tab.

2. Specify the **Application mode** option. If this option is checked, the CRM web client will be opened in a browser window without the menu, navigation, and command bars.

3. Click on **OK** to save your changes.

Outlook

To configure the Outlook synchronization system settings, perform the following steps:

1. Click on the **Outlook** tab.

2. Specify the following options:

    ○ **Set e-mail promotion options for Microsoft Dynamics CRM for Outlook**: Specify how e-mail messages will be handled: perform checks as e-mail messages are received, set the interval for tracking incoming e-mail messages, and set the interval for sending outbound CRM e-mail messages.

    ○ **Set whether users can schedule synchronization in Microsoft Dynamics CRM for Outlook**: Specify the minimum time interval between synchronizations and whether users can specify a personal interval or not.

    ○ **Set whether users can update their local data in the background in Microsoft Dynamics CRM for Outlook**: Specify the minimum time interval between background offline data updates and whether users can specify a personal interval or not.

    ○ **Set schedule for address book synchronization in Microsoft Dynamics CRM for Outlook**: Specify the minimum time interval between address book synchronizations and whether users can specify a personal interval or not.

    ○ **Set whether users see "Get the Outlook client" in the Message Bar**: Specify whether the CRM for Outlook client advertisement is broadcast in the CRM web client.

3. Click on **OK** to save your changes.

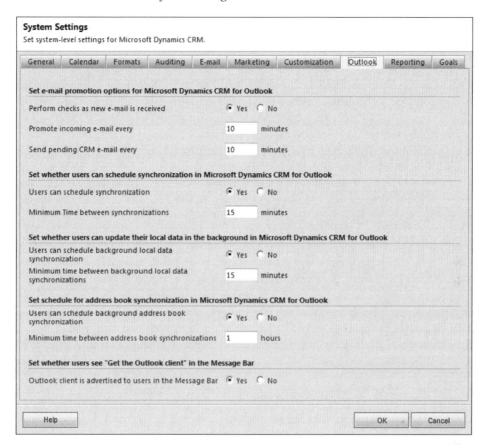

Outlook synchronization settings

The Outlook synchronization settings is an important area for Microsoft customers deploying the CRM for Outlook client. Some of the Outlook synchronization settings are configured in the **System Settings** area and some additional options can be specified by the user in the **Personal Options** area. It's important to know how these two groups of settings affect the Outlook synchronization.

See the *Understanding CRM for Outlook settings* section discussed later in this chapter foran overview of the **Personal Options** settings available to users.

Reporting

To configure the reporting system settings, perform the following steps:

1. Click on the **Reporting** tab.
2. Specify the following options:
    - **Specify report categories**: You can associate a report with one or more categories so that you can, for example, define a reports view based on a report category filter. The report categories available while publishing or modifying a report are defined in this system settings tab.
    - **Default Value**: Optionally, you can specify one of the report categories to be the default reporting category associated with the new reports.

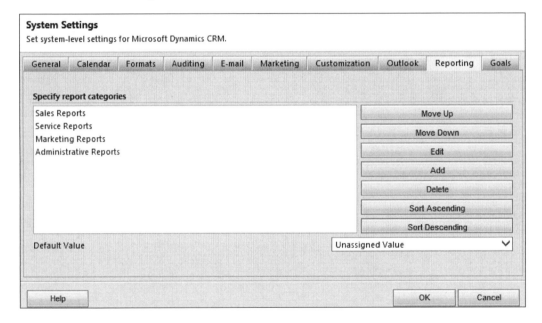

Goals

To configure the goal system settings, follow these steps:

1. Click on the **Goals** tab.

2. Specify the following options:

   ○ **Days after the goal end date when the rollup will stop**: The system will recalculate goal attainment regularly during the goal period and for a specified period of time after the end of the goal period. For example, last year's sales revenue will be recalculated every day during the year and for 30 days after the end of the year. Use this setting to specify how many days after the end of the goal period that goal attainment should be recalculated.

   ○ **Roll-up recurrence frequency**: Use this setting to specify how often goal attainment should be recalculated.

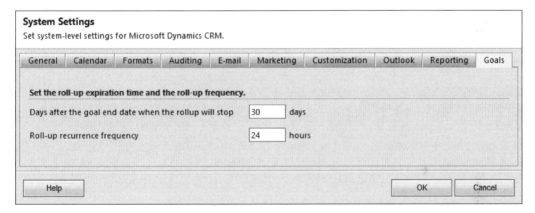

Understanding CRM for Outlook settings

Microsoft Dynamics CRM 2011 for Microsoft Office Outlook client, known as **CRM for Outlook**, is an add-in for Microsoft Outlook that provides a number of features:

- Access to Microsoft Dynamics CRM records and features from Microsoft Outlook.

- E-mail messages sent and received through Outlook can be tracked in CRM and associated with CRM records.

- E-mail messages created in CRM can be delivered through Outlook.
- Contacts can be synchronized between CRM and a user's Outlook contacts folder.
- Appointments can be synchronized between CRM and a user's Outlook calendar.
- Tasks, phone calls, faxes, and letters can be synchronized between CRM and a user's Outlook tasks list.
- E-mail addresses of CRM leads, accounts, and contacts can be synchronized with a user's Outlook address book.
- CRM for Outlook with Offline Access provides an offline client that can be used without a network connection and then can be synchronized with CRM once a network connection is re-established.

Additionally, CRM for Outlook is required for some CRM features such as:

- Sending Direct E-mail via Mail Merge
- Accessing a dynamic Excel workbook exported from CRM
- Previewing records and the conditional formatting of records in a grid

CRM for Outlook settings

Some of the CRM for Outlook settings are configured in the **System Settings** area by the system administrator and other settings can be configured by the user in the user's **Personal Options** area in CRM for Outlook.

CRM System Settings

The following sections discuss the settings related to CRM for Outlook. These settings are configured in the **System Settings** area.

- The **General** tab under **System Settings**:
  - Blocked file extensions for attachments

- The **E-mail** tab under **System Settings**:
  - Process e-mail only for approved users
  - Process e-mail only for approved queues
  - Use tracking token and the tracking options
  - Use smart matching and the smart matching options
  - Track e-mails sent between users as two activities

- ○ Use secure frames to restrict e-mail message content
- ○ Allow messages with the unresolved e-mail recipients to be sent
- ○ Maximum file size

- The **Outlook** tab under **System Settings**:

- ○ Perform checks as new e-mail is received
- ○ Promote incoming e-mail every 10 minutes
- ○ Send pending e-mail every 10 minutes
- ○ Users can schedule synchronization
- ○ Minimum time between synchronizations
- ○ Users can schedule background local data synchronization
- ○ Minimum time between background local data synchronizations
- ○ Users can schedule background address book synchronization
- ○ Minimum time between address book synchronizations

CRM for Outlook Personal Options

Detailed knowledge of the **Personal Options** area of CRM for Outlook is not required for MB2-866. However, it is possible that you may be asked a question that tests your understanding of the difference between the configuration options available in **System Settings** in the CRM web client and the **Personal Options** settings in the CRM for Outlook client.

The following settings related to CRM for Outlook are configured in the **Personal Options** area in CRM for Outlook by each user:

- The **General** tab under the CRM for Outlook Personal Options:
  - ○ Use the Microsoft Dynamics CRM forms instead of standard Outlook forms for appointment, contact, task, and e-mail

- The **Synchronization** tab under the CRM for Outlook Personal Options:
  - ○ The synchronization filters that determine the data synchronized with Outlook
  - ○ Update the **Company** field on the Outlook contacts with the name of the contact's parent account in CRM
  - ○ Synchronize CRM with Outlook every 15 minutes (depending on the minimum time interval between synchronizations setting in the **System Settings** area)

- The **E-mail** tab under the CRM for Outlook Personal Options:
  - ○ Allow Microsoft Dynamics CRM to send e-mail using Microsoft Dynamics CRM for Outlook
  - ○ Check incoming e-mail in Outlook and determine whether an e-mail should be linked and saved as a CRM record or not
  - ○ Track e-mail messages in response to the CRM e-mail, or track e-mail messages from CRM leads, accounts, and contacts, or track e-mail messages from all records that are e-mail-enabled
  - ○ Create contacts or leads from the sender or organizer of tracked e-mail messages and meetings

- The **Address Book** tab under the CRM for Outlook Personal Options:
  - ○ Match only against contacts synchronized to Microsoft Dynamics CRM, or match all contacts in Microsoft Dynamics CRM
  - ○ Do not match other record types, or match only the items I own, or match all items in Microsoft Dynamics CRM
  - ○ Record types synchronized to the Outlook address book

- The **Local Data** tab under the CRM for Outlook Personal Options:
  - ○ Update local data every 15 minutes (depending on the minimum time interval between synchronizations setting in the **System Settings** area)
  - ○ Enable duplicate detection during offline to online synchronization

Exportable settings

When you export a solution, you have an option to include the current system settings of the CRM organization so that the same system settings can be applied in the target organization.

Solutions are described in more detail in *Chapter 8, Solutions*.

However, there are some differences between the set of system settings that are exportable in a solution, and those available for configuration in the **System Settings** area.

System settings exported in a solution

The following settings from the **System Settings** area can be exported in a solution:

- Calendar
- Customization
- E-mail Tracking
- General
- Marketing
- Outlook Synchronization

System settings not exported in a solution

The following settings from the **System Settings** area cannot be exported in a solution:

- Formats
- Auditing
- Reporting
- Goals

Additional settings exported in a solution

The following additional settings, that are not part of the **System Settings** area, can also be exported in a solution:

- Auto-Numbering
- Relationship Roles
- ISV Config

Auto-numbering

To configure the auto-numbering system settings, follow these steps:

1. In the navigation pane, click on **Settings**.
2. Click on **Administration** and then select **Auto-Numbering** in the **Administration** area.

3. For each entity that supports auto-numbering, specify the following options:

   ○ **Prefix**: Specify the letters that will prepend the auto-number

   ○ **Suffix Length**: Specify the number of random characters that will append the auto-number

4. Click on **OK** to save your changes.

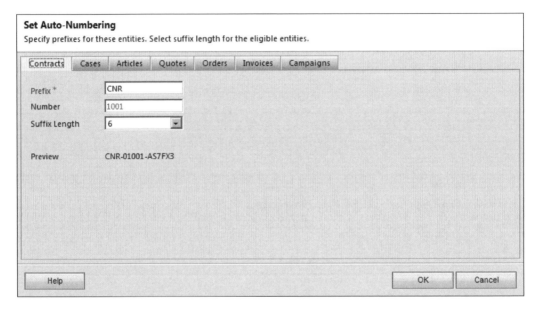

Relationship Roles

Relationship Roles is a feature from the previous versions of Microsoft Dynamics CRM and is not used in Microsoft Dynamics CRM 2011 unless the system has been upgraded from Microsoft Dynamics CRM 4.0.

Any relationship roles that have been configured can be exported as the system settings when exporting a CRM 2011 solution.

ISV Config

ISV Config is a feature from the previous versions of Microsoft Dynamics CRM and is not used in Microsoft Dynamics CRM 2011.

The exception to this is where changes have been made to the appearance and behavior of the service calendar by using the method described in the Microsoft Dynamics CRM SDK available at `http://msdn.microsoft.com/en-us/library/gg309501.aspx`.

Summary

Microsoft Dynamics CRM 2011 provides a wide range of system settings that can be customized to meet your business requirements. System settings are configurable settings that apply to the entire system.

Some of the CRM for Outlook settings are configured in the **System Settings** area by the system administrator and other settings can be configured by the user in the user's **Personal Options** area in CRM for Outlook.

Most — but not all — of the system settings can be exported in a solution. It is important to know which settings and customizations are not included within a solution and need to be managed separately.

Test your knowledge

Q. 1 Which one of the following settings can be configured In the **System Settings** area?

1. Currency precision

2. Pricing decimal precision

3. Currency exchange rates

4. Currency field custom precision

5. Currency symbol used for each currency

Q. 2   Which of the following system settings cannot be exported in a solution (select all that apply)?

1. Auditing
2. Formats
3. Marketing
4. Reporting
5. Synchronization

Q. 3   Which of the following settings related to CRM for Outlook are not configured in the **System Settings** area?

1. User filters that specify which contacts synchronize between CRM and Outlook
2. Perform checks as new e-mail messages are received
3. Update the Company field on the Outlook contacts with the parent account
4. Use smart matching to associate replies to the original e-mail
5. Interval between sending pending e-mail messages

3
Configuring the Organization Structure

The organization structure is a combination of business units, security roles, teams, and users used for providing or denying access to certain features and records. The main purpose of the organization structure is to meet your security requirements.

In this chapter we will cover:

- The organization structure
- Business units
- Users
- Teams
- Security roles and privileges
- Other security features

So let's get on with it...

The organization structure

The **organization structure** in Microsoft Dynamics CRM refers to the hierarchy of business units, users, and teams configured within your organization. A **business unit** represents a part of your organization that has security requirements distinct from another part. A **user** is someone (usually employed by your organization) who needs access to the CRM system. A **team** is a group of users who work together.

Each user and team must belong to one business unit. All the records owned by that user or team are also considered to be in that business unit.

Best practice

Keep the organization structure as simple as possible while meeting your organization's security requirements, industry regulations, and local laws.

Planning the organization structure

It is a good idea to plan your organization structure and consider the business units, users, teams, and security roles before creating them.

Business units, users, teams, and security roles can all be renamed if required, but using short, descriptive names is preferred so that mergers, acquisitions, divestments, restructuring, or rebranding doesn't lead to lots of organization structure changes in your CRM system.

Business units

A **business unit** represents a part of your organization that has security requirements distinct from another part. Business units could correspond to your organization's divisions or departments, but the business units configured in Microsoft Dynamics CRM do not necessarily need to match the business units shown in your organization chart. Distinct business units only need to be created in CRM where distinct security requirements exist.

In this section we will learn about:

- The root business unit
- Managing the business units

The root business unit

The **root business unit** is the ultimate parent business unit in the organization structure. It is created by the CRM Server setup program, when CRM is installed with all server roles or by the CRM Deployment Manager, when a new CRM organization is deployed.

The root business unit has the following properties:

- It can be renamed
- It cannot be disabled or deleted
- It cannot have a parent business unit

Managing the business units

By default, you need to have a System Administrator security role to manage business units (users with the CEO-Business Manager security role can also manage business units, but it's not a good idea to let your CEO do this).

How to create a new business unit

To create a new business unit, follow these steps:

1. In the navigation pane, click on **Settings**.

2. In the **System** group, click on **Administration**, and then click on **Business Units**.

3. Click on **New**.

4. In the **Business Unit: New** form, provide the required information:

    ◦ **Name**: Enter a unique name for the new business unit.

    ◦ **Parent Business**: Use the lookup field to associate the new business unit with its parent business unit.

5. Click on **Save and Close**.

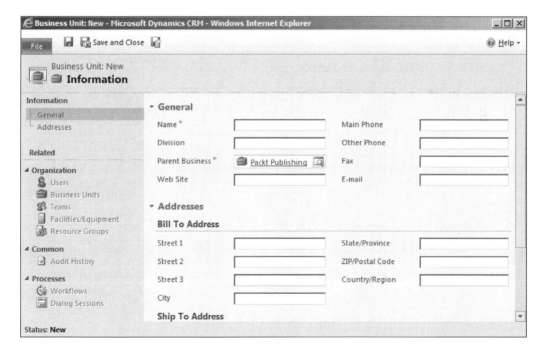

When a business unit is created, a new team is created with the same name. When a user is assigned to the business unit, that user will also be added to the team.

How to rename a business unit

In Microsoft Dynamics CRM 2011, business units, including the root business unit, can be renamed. When a business unit is renamed, its corresponding team is also renamed.

To rename a business unit, follow these steps:

1. Navigate to the **Business Units** grid.
2. Open the business unit that you want to rename.
3. Change the name of the business unit by using the **Name** field.
4. Click on **Save and Close**.

How to change a business unit's parent business unit

We can reorganize our CRM organization structure by changing a business unit's parent business unit.

To change a business unit's parent business unit, follow these steps:

1. Navigate to the **Business Units** grid.
2. Select the business unit for which you want to change the parent.
3. On the toolbar, select **More Actions** and then select **Change Parent Business**.
4. In the **Change Parent Business** dialog, use the lookup to find the new parent business unit.
5. Click on **OK**.

There are some constraints when changing parent business units:

- When a business unit's parent is changed, all of its children (business units, users, and teams) move with it
- All other business units must have a parent business unit
- You cannot create circular relationships between business units

How to disable and enable a business unit

All business units, except the root parent business unit, can be disabled. This can be useful for managing organizational restructures.

Disabling a business unit

To disable a business unit, follow these steps:

1. Navigate to the **Business Units** grid.
2. Select the business unit that you want to disable.
3. On the toolbar, select **More Actions** and then select **Disable**.
4. Click on **OK**.

There are some important considerations when disabling business units:

- No data associated with the disabled business unit is deleted
- Disabling a business unit also disables any child business units
- Disabling a business unit does not disable the business unit's users, but users of a disabled business unit will not be able to log in until the business unit is enabled or the user is reassigned to an enabled business unit
- Disabling a business unit does not disable the business unit's teams, but users that rely on the team for access to the security privileges or records will not have access to those privileges or records
- You cannot assign the business units, users, or teams to a disabled business unit

Enabling a business unit

To enable a business unit, follow these steps:

1. Navigate to the **Business Units** grid.
2. Select the **Inactive Business Units** view.
3. Select the business unit that you want to enable.
4. On the toolbar, select **More Actions** and then select **Enable**.
5. Click on **OK**.

There are some important considerations when enabling business units:

- When you enable a business unit, any child business units will also be enabled

- Any users assigned to the re-enabled business unit will be able to log in again

- Disabling or enabling a business unit does not disable or enable users associated with the business unit

How to delete a business unit

All business units, except the root parent business unit, can be deleted. This can be useful for managing organizational restructures.

To delete a business unit, follow these steps:

1. Navigate to the **Business Units** grid.
2. Select the **Inactive Business Units** view.
3. Select the business unit that you want to disable.
4. On the toolbar, click on the **Delete** button.
5. Click on **OK**.

There are some important considerations when deleting business units:

- An enabled business unit cannot be deleted. Business units must be disabled before they can be deleted.

- A business unit cannot be deleted if it has child business units. Child business units must be reassigned before the business unit can be deleted.

- A business unit cannot be deleted if it has users or teams associated with it (except for the business unit's default team). Users and teams must be reassigned before the business unit can be deleted.

- If these conditions are satisfied, the business unit will be permanently deleted and this action cannot be undone. For this reason, it is more common to disable business units that are no longer required rather than deleting them.

Need to know — business units

Your MB2-866 exam is likely to cover the procedures and requirements for (as well as consequences of) creating, disabling, enabling, re-parenting, and deleting business units. It is recommended that you understand this section and practice the procedures in your CRM 2011 organization.

Users

A **user** is someone, usually employed by your organization, who needs access to the CRM system.

In this section we will cover:

- Introduction to user management
- Creating and managing users

Introduction to user management

In this section we will cover:

- Importance of managing users
- Authentication
- Licensing

Importance of managing users

Depending on the number of users in your deployment, user management can be an occasional task for the CRM system administrator or a continuous workload for the CRM system administration team.

There are several reasons why user management is important:

- Maintaining users in the correct business unit and with the correct security roles ensures that they have access only to the privileges and records that they are entitled to according to your security policies.

- Maintaining the access modes and license types for your users and purchasing the appropriate client access licenses ensures that your organization complies with its Microsoft license agreements.

- Maintaining the correct manager for each user ensures that any escalations will work correctly. For example, you might have a workflow rule that notifies a user's manager when one of the user's cases or opportunities meet certain criteria.

- Maintaining teams correctly can simplify the task of assigning security roles to specific users and supports the sharing of records between users.

- Reports are often based on business units and/or teams. If users are not assigned to the correct business units or teams, management reports will be incorrect.

Authentication

In order to log in to Microsoft Dynamics CRM, a user must have a user account in the CRM organization and must be authenticated by an authentication service.

Different authentication services are used depending upon the type of deployment, however, these are not within the scope of the MB2-866 exam. This book assumes you are working with an on-premise deployment and using Active Directory as your authentication service.

Deployment and authentication options

The Microsoft Dynamics CRM 2011 Implementation Guide provides information for planning, deploying, and supporting the alternative deployment and authentication options (http://www.microsoft.com/en-us/download/details.aspx?id=3621).

In a typical on-premise deployment, when the user opens the Microsoft Dynamics CRM web client or Microsoft Dynamics CRM for Outlook, the user's network login credentials will be automatically passed to Active Directory for authentication. This is known as **single sign-on**.

Licensing

Different access modes and license types depending on the type of deployment are available.

Need to know—licensing

With many different deployment options, access modes, and license types available, we could write a whole book about the Microsoft Dynamics CRM licensing. The information provided in this section describes what you typically need to know for the MB2-866 exam.

Access modes

The access modes available within an on-premise deployment are as follows:

- **Read-Write**: This is the typical access mode assigned to most users. Users with the read-write access type can work with all records according to their security privileges.

- **Administrative**: This access mode provides users with access only to the **Settings** area and it does not consume a license.

- **Read**: Users with this access mode can read the records according to their security privileges, but cannot create, update, or delete any records.

Full or limited client access licenses need to be purchased for all users with a read-write access mode. Limited client access licenses need to be purchased for all users with a read access mode.

License types

The **client access license (CAL)** types available within an on-premise deployment are as follows:

- **Full**: This is the license type assigned to most users. Users with the full license type can create, read, update, and delete all records according to their security privileges.
- **Limited**: This license type allows users to work with a subset of entities.
- **Device Full**: Devices with the device-full license type can be shared by users to work with all records according to their security privileges.
- **Device Limited**: Devices with the device-limited license type can be shared by users to work with a subset of records.
- **Employee Self-Service**: This license type provides limited read and write access to entities through a custom user interface that accesses the CRM API.

External connector license

For an on-premise deployment, client access licenses are required for each named user. Microsoft considers all employees and people acting like an employee (agency staff, affiliates, contractors, or consultants) to be users, and they each need their own CAL.

Client access licenses are not required for people who are not employees and who access the CRM features and data through a custom user interface such as a customer, partner, or supplier portal. Instead, an external connector license for each CRM server in the deployment is required.

Creating and managing users

This section describes how to create new user accounts and manage existing users in Microsoft Dynamics CRM 2011.

How to create a user

To create a new user, follow these steps:

1. In the navigation pane, click on **Settings**.
2. In the **System** group, click on **Administration** and then click on **Users**.

3. On the ribbon, click on the **New** button.

4. Enter the new user's information. Important fields are as follows:

    ◦ **Domain Logon Name**: This is the user's Active Directory domain logon name, for example, domain name/username. When you enter a valid domain logon name and tab off this field, some information about the user will be retrieved from Active Directory and displayed in the user record.

    ◦ **Primary E-mail**: This is the e-mail address used to send and receive e-mails from CRM. By default, the primary e-mail address for each user needs to be approved by a system administrator, using the **Approve E-mail** button on the user form toolbar, before e-mail messages can be sent or received by using the CRM E-mail Router.

    ◦ **Business Unit**: It is important to set the user's business unit correctly in order to comply with your organization's security policies.

    ◦ **E-mail access type – Incoming** and **E-mail access type – Outgoing**: The e-mail access type determines whether the user can send e-mail from CRM or not. There are following options available for these fields:

        None: e-mail messages will not be sent from or tracked in CRM.

        Microsoft Dynamics CRM for Outlook: e-mail messages will be sent from and tracked in CRM by using CRM for Outlook.

        E-mail Router: e-mail messages will be sent from and tracked in CRM by using the CRM E-mail Router.

        Forward Mailbox: e-mail messages will be sent from and tracked in CRM by using the **Forward Mailbox** option with the CRM E-mail Router.

    ◦ **Access Mode** and **License Type**: Select the appropriate access mode and license type for the user, and ensure that appropriate client access licenses have been purchased.

    ◦ **Manager**: Specifying the correct manager for each user ensures that any escalations will work correctly. For example, you might have a workflow rule that notifies a user's manager when one of the user's cases or opportunities meet specified criteria.

5. Click on **Save and Close**.

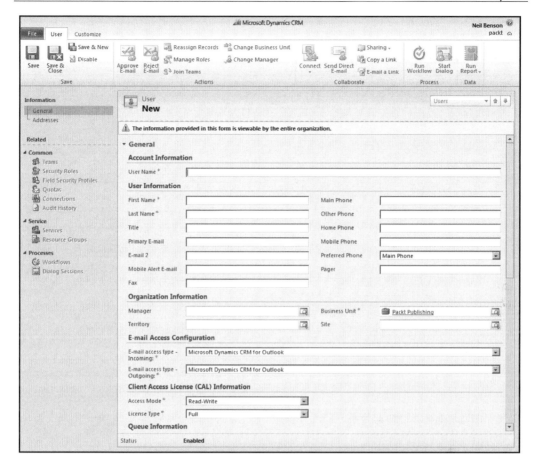

A new user will not be able to log in to CRM until you have assigned at least one security role to the user's account.

How to create multiple users

Microsoft Dynamics CRM provides a wizard for adding multiple users at once. The **Multiple New Users** wizard can be used to create batches of new users where each user in a batch has the same business unit, security roles, access mode, and license type.

To create multiple users, follow these steps:

1. Navigate to the **Users** area.
2. In the **Users** ribbon, click on **New Multiple Users**.

3. In the **Add Users** pop-up window, under the **Select Business Unit** section, select the business unit to which the batch of users will be assigned.

4. Click on **Next**.

5. In the **Select Security Roles** section, select one or more security roles that will be assigned to the batch of users.

6. Click on **Next**.

7. In the **Select Access and License Type** section, select specific options for the following fields:

   ° **Access Type**: Choose **Read-Write**, **Administrative**, or **Read**

   ° **License Type**: Select **Full, Limited, Device Full** or **Device Limited**

   ° **E-mail Access Configuration**: Under this field, for **E-mail access type – Incoming,** you can select **None, Microsoft Dynamics CRM for Outlook, E-mail Router,** or **Forward Mailbox**. For **E-mail access type – Outgoing,** you can select **None, Microsoft Dynamics CRM for Outlook,** or **E-mail Router**.

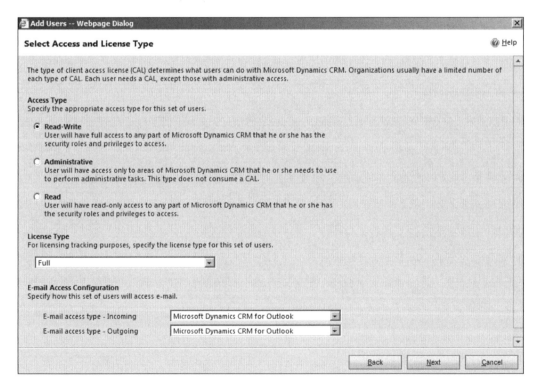

8. Click on **Next**.

9. In the **Select Domain or Group** section, choose:

    ° **Select users from all trusted domains and groups** to add users from any group, domain, or tree in your organization's Active Directory forest

    ° **Select users from the following domain or groups** to browse to a specific group in your organization's Active Directory forest

10. Click on **Next**.

11. In the **Select Users** section, type or paste the names of the users to be added in this batch. You can use the users' full names or domain/login names separated with semicolons, or use the **Lookup** feature to find the users.

12. Click on **Create New Users**.

13. Once the wizard has finished adding the batch of new users, click on **Add More Users** to create another batch of new users, or click on **Close** to close the wizard.

How to disable a user

If a user leaves your organization, it is recommended that the user's CRM user record should be disabled rather than deleting it. This preserves data for historical purposes.

To disable a user, follow these steps:

1. Navigate to the **Users** area.

2. Select the user that you want to disable.

3. In the **Users** ribbon, click on **Disable**.

4. Click on **OK** to confirm deactivation.

There are some important considerations regarding disabled users:

- Disabled users cannot log in to CRM

- Disabled users do not consume a client access license

- Records cannot be assigned to a disabled user

- Published processes (workflows or dialogs) owned by a disabled user will not work until the workflows are reassigned to an active user or the disabled user is re-enabled

How to enable a user

To enable a disabled user, follow these steps:

1. Navigate to the **Users** area.
2. Select the **Inactive Users** view.
3. Select the user that you want to enable.
4. In the **Users** ribbon, click on **Enable**.
5. Click on **OK** to confirm re-activation.

There are some important considerations regarding enabled users:

- Enabled users consume a client access license
- Enabling a disabled user does not affect the user's security roles

How to reassign a user's records to another user

You may want to use the **Reassign Records** feature to reassign a user's record to another user.

To reassign a user's records to another user, follow these steps:

1. Navigate to the **Users** area.
2. Open the user's record.
3. In the **Users** ribbon, click on **Reassign Records**.
4. In the **Reassign Records** pop-up window, select **Assign to me** if you want to be the new owner of the user's records, otherwise, select **Assign to another user or team** and specify the other user or team in the lookup field.
5. Click on **OK**.

> ### Beware — Reassign Records
>
>
>
> The **Reassign Records** feature reassigns all records regardless of the record state. This means that completed activities, resolved cases, qualified and disqualified leads, won opportunities, inactive accounts, and contacts will all be reassigned. In most situations, this is not desirable, so the **Reassign Records** feature should be used with care.

How to assign a security role to a user

A new user will not be able to log in to CRM until you have assigned at least one security role.

To assign a security role to a user, follow these steps:

1. Navigate to the **Users** area.

2. Select the user or users that you want to assign a security role to.

3. On the ribbon, click on the **Manage Role** button.

4. In the **Confirm Security Role Assignment** dialog, select the security role or required security roles.

5. Click on **OK**.

How to assign a user to a team

To assign a user to a team, follow these steps:

1. Navigate to the **Users** area.
2. Open the user record.
3. On the **Users** ribbon, click on the **Join Teams** button.
4. In the **Lookup Records** pop-up window, select the required teams.
5. Click on **OK**.

There are some important considerations regarding reassigning records:

- You cannot assign a user to any of the default business unit teams
- A user assigned to a team will be granted all the security privileges associated with any security roles assigned to the team

Teams

A **team** is a group of users who work together. Teams can own records.

In this section we will cover:

- Introduction to teams
- Default business unit teams
- Managing teams

Introduction to teams

Teams is an optional feature in Microsoft Dynamics CRM 2011. However, there are a number of scenarios where teams are useful:

- **Owning unallocated records**: Imagine you have a group of prospect accounts that you don't want to assign to a user in the sales department yet because it would clutter the user's views and reports. You can assign those accounts to a team before they are later claimed by a sales person and the account is reassigned to a sales user.
- **Sharing records with a group of users**: Imagine you frequently share records with the same group of users in different business units. By creating a team and adding those users to it, you can now share records with the team to achieve the same result with fewer clicks.

- **Assigning a security role in one business unit to users in another business unit**: Imagine that users in each region can only work with cases in their own region. An upsurge in support cases in region A can be managed by users in region B by assigning some of the users in region B to a team in region A that enables them to work with region A's cases.

There are some important considerations regarding teams:

- Each team must be assigned to a business unit and an administrator user
- Users can be a member of any team regardless of the business unit of the team or the user
- Sharing a record with a team shares it with all the users in the team
- Assigning a security role to a team assigns the security role to all the users in the team based on the business unit of the team, not the users

Default business unit teams

A default team is created for each business unit in your organization structure and all users in the business unit are assigned to the default business unit team.

There are some important considerations regarding default business unit teams:

- They cannot be deleted or disabled
- They can be renamed only by renaming the business unit
- They cannot be assigned to another business unit
- You cannot manually manage the team's members

Managing teams

Teams can be managed by the CRM system administrator or any user with sufficient security privileges.

How to create a team

To create a team, follow these steps:

1. Navigate to the **Teams** area.
2. Click on **New**.

3. In the **Team** form enter the following information:
   ° **Team Name**: The name must be unique within the business unit
   ° **Business Unit**: By default, this will be the root parent business unit
   ° **Administrator**: The administrator must be a user in the same business unit as the team
   ° **Default Queue**: If you do not specify a queue, a queue will automatically be created with the same name as the team

4. Click on **Save and Close**.

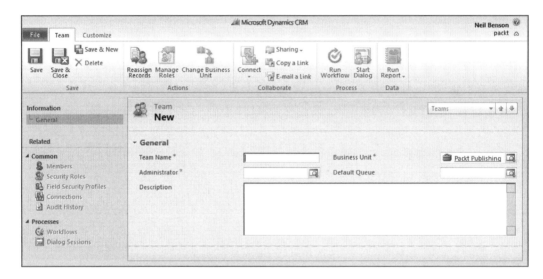

How to add users to a team

To add users to a team, follow these steps:

1. Navigate to the **Teams** area.
2. Open the team to which you want to add users.
3. In the **Team** form, click on the **Members** area.
4. In the team form ribbon, click on **Add Members**.
5. In the **Lookup Records** pop-up window, search and select the users you want to add to the team.
6. Click on **Add** to add the selected users to the **Selected records** area.
7. Click on **OK**.
8. Close the **Team** form.

How to remove users from a team

To remove users from a team, follow these steps:

1. Navigate to the **Teams** area.
2. Open the team from which you want to remove users.
3. In the **Team** form, click on the **Members** area.
4. Select the users that you want to remove.
5. In the team form ribbon, click on **Remove**.
6. In the **Confirm User Removal** pop-up window, click on **OK** to confirm.
7. Close the **Team** form.

How to add teams to a user

As well as adding users to a team from within the **Team** form, you can also add teams to a user from within the **User** form.

To add teams to a user, follow these steps:

1. Navigate to the **Users** area.
2. Open the user to whom you want to add the teams.
3. In the **User** form, click on the **Teams** area.
4. In the **Users** ribbon, click on **Add Existing Team**.
5. In the **Lookup Records** pop-up window, search and select the teams that you want to add to the user.
6. Click on **Add** to add the selected teams to the **Selected records** area.
7. Click on **OK**.
8. Close the **User** form.

How to assign a security role to a team

Assigning a user to a team that has a security role and is in a different business unit will enable the user to work with all the records in that business unit (according to the privileges granted by the team's security role).

To add a security role to a team, follow these steps:

1. Navigate to the **Teams** area.
2. Open the team to which you want to add a security role.

3. In the **Team** form, click on the **Security Roles** area.

4. In the security roles grid toolbar, click on **Manage Roles**.

5. In the **Manage Team Roles** pop-up window, select the security role that you want to add to the team.

6. Click on **OK** to add the selected security role to team.

7. Close the **Team** form.

Users in the team will have the security privileges granted to them by the team's security role in the team's business unit in addition to the security roles directly assigned to the user in the user's business unit.

How to remove a security role from a team

To remove a security role from a team, follow these steps:

1. Navigate to the **Teams** area.

2. Open the team from which you want to remove a security role.

3. In the **Team** form, click on the **Security Roles** area.

4. Select the security role that you want to remove from the team.

5. In the security roles grid toolbar, click on **Remove Roles**.

6. In the **Confirm Role Removal** pop-up window, click on **OK**.

7. Close the **Team** form.

How to share records with a team

Sharing records with a team provides the users in the team with the selected privileges for the shared records.

To share records with a team, follow these steps:

1. Select the records that you want to share.

2. In the ribbon, click on **Share**.

3. In the **Who would you like to share the selected records with?** pop-up window, click on **Add User/Team**.

4. In the **Lookup Records** pop-up window, change **Look** for value to **Team**, and then search and select the team with which you want to share the records.

5. Click on **Add** to move the team to the **Selected records** area.

6. Click on **OK**.

7. Select the privileges that you want to provide to the team members. You can select from **Read**, **Write**, **Delete**, **Append**, **Assign**, and **Share**.

8. Click on **OK**.

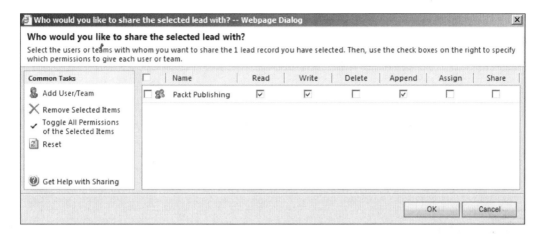

There are some important considerations regarding sharing records with a team:

- The user or team must have at least user-level read privileges for the entity that you want to share before sharing allows access. So, you cannot share an account with a user or team who cannot read any accounts.

- The **Append sharing** privilege is the equivalent of the combined **Append** and **Append To** security privileges that are assigned through a security role.

- Sharing a record with a default business unit team shares the record with all the users in that business unit.

How to unshare records with a team

Unsharing records with a team denies the users in the team with the previously selected privileges for the shared records.

To unshare records with a team, follow these steps:

1. Select the records that you want to unshare.

2. In the ribbon, click on **Share**.

3. In the **Who would you like to share the selected records with?** pop-up window, select the team with which you want to unshared the records.

4. Click on **Remove Selected Items**.

5. Click on **OK**.

How to delete a team

To delete a team, follow these steps:

1. Navigate to the **Teams** area.
2. Select the team that you want to delete.
3. In the **Teams** ribbon, click on **Delete**.
4. In the **Confirm Deletion** pop-up window, click on **OK**.

There are some important considerations regarding deleting the teams:

- You cannot delete a default business unit team.
- You cannot delete any team that owns records. If the team owns records you will need to delete or reassign the records before you can delete the team.
- You do not need to delete users or security roles from a team before deleting the team.

Security roles and privileges

A **security role** defines a collection of security privileges, and a security privilege provides access to an entity or feature. The security features of Microsoft Dynamics CRM 2011—comprised of business units, security roles, and privileges—provide users and teams with access to records or features required to perform their jobs without providing them access to restricted records or features according to your organization's security policy.

Introduction to security roles

Security roles define a collection of entity- and task-based security privileges that can be assigned to users or teams.

Standard security roles

When a new Microsoft Dynamics CRM 2011 organization is deployed, 14 standard security roles are included with it. These security roles provide entity- and task-based security privileges for typical job roles in a business.

The standard security roles are as follows:

- **CEO-Business Manager**: Provides organization-level access to all records and access to almost all task-based privileges with the exception of customization privileges
- **CSR Manager**: Provides organization-level access to customer service records and access to a significant number of task-based privileges
- **Customer Service Representative**: Provides organization-level access to most customer service records and access to some task-based privileges
- **Delegate**: Provides a single task-based privilege called **Act on behalf of another user**
- **Marketing Manager**: Provides business-unit- or organization-level access to most records and access to some task-based privileges
- **Marketing Professional**: Provides business-unit- or organization-level access to most records and access to some task-based privileges
- **Sales Manager**: Provides business-unit- or organization-level access to most records and access to some task-based privileges including pricing override privileges
- **Salesperson**: Provides user- or business-unit-level access to most records and access to some task-based privileges
- **Schedule Manager**: Provides access to most core records and some task-based privileges including most service management privileges
- **Scheduler**: Provides access to most core records and some task-based privileges including some service management privileges
- **System Administrator**: Has organization-level access to all system and custom entities and full access to all task-based security privileges (and cannot be customized or deleted)
- **System Customizer**: Provides some access to most records and some access to task-based privileges including customization privileges
- **Vice President of Marketing**: Provides business-unit- or organization-level access to most records and access to some task-based privileges including pricing override privileges

- **Vice President of Sales**: Provides business-unit- or organization-level access to most records and access to some task-based privileges including pricing override privileges

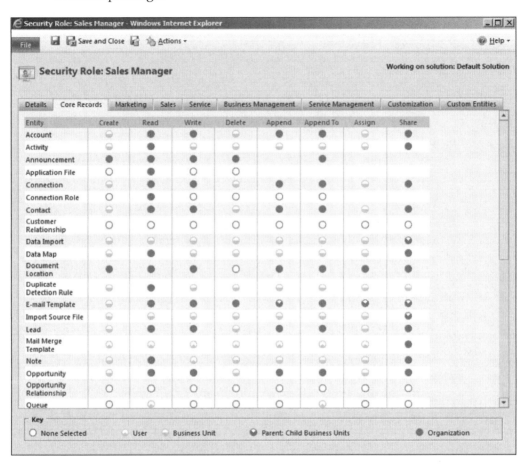

Customizing the standard security roles

The standard security roles provide a robust set of security roles that can be used without modification. However, to meet your organization's security requirements, you may need to create custom security roles. The best practice is to create a copy of one of the standard security roles and to modify the copy to meet your organization's unique needs.

Security roles and custom entities

By default, none of the security roles—except the System Administrator security role—provide access to any custom entities you create. So, you will have to customize existing security roles or create new security roles and assign them to your users or teams before they can work with your custom entities.

Business units and inherited security roles

Security roles must be assigned to a business unit and can be assigned to a business unit at any level in your organization hierarchy. Security roles assigned to any parent business unit are automatically inherited by all its child business units. When you create a new child business unit, all the security roles are copied from its parent business unit.

It is possible—but not recommended—to have different security roles with different security privileges, but with the same name assigned to different business units. Instead, it is recommended that all security roles are assigned to the root parent business unit.

Inherited security roles cannot be modified or deleted. Instead, you can modify or delete the security role in the parent business unit. When you modify or delete the security role, this modification or deletion is cascaded to all inherited security roles.

Applying security roles to users and teams

This section describes how security roles can be applied to users and teams.

Security roles and users

After a new user account has been created, it must be assigned at least one security role before the user can log in to Microsoft Dynamics CRM 2011. The user's security role must belong to the same business unit as the user.

A user can be assigned more than one security role and is granted a combination of all the security privileges conferred by all their security roles. It is important to note that security privileges granted by security roles are additive. This means that if one security role grants no access to a custom entity but another security role grants business-unit-level access to the same custom entity, the user is granted business-unit-level access to the custom entity.

It is common practice to create a small number of job-tailored security roles (often copied from the standard security roles) and an additional number of security roles that grant one or two task-based security privileges, such as Go Offline and Go Mobile, so that you can control exactly which users have to be granted those privileges. The standard Delegate security role is a good example of this practice.

The User Summary report

The standard **User Summary report** is a matrix-style report that describes the security roles assigned to each user grouped by business unit.

How to run the User Summary report

To run the User Summary report, follow these steps:

1. Navigate to the **Reports** area.

2. Double-click on the **User Summary** report.

3. In the **Report Filtering Criteria** screen, provide any filter criteria that you want to apply to the report, or leave blank if you want to run the report for all records.

4. Click on **Run Report**.

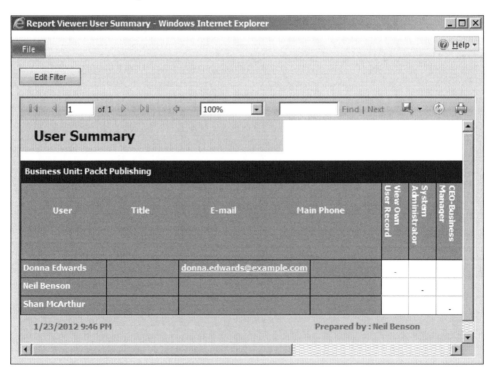

Reassigning users

When a user is reassigned to a different business unit, CRM will remove the user's existing security roles. So, it is important to assign new security roles to the user after assigning the user to a new business unit, otherwise the user will be unable to log in to CRM.

Security roles and teams

In Microsoft Dynamics CRM 2011, it is possible to assign security roles to a team. Assigning security roles to teams provides a powerful method for creating exceptions to the normal user-based security roles in order to meet your organization's security requirements.

Assigning a security role to a team grants all the users in that team with the security privileges specified by the security role in the team's business unit regardless of the users' business units.

For example, imagine this scenario. A user has a security role that grants the business-unit-level read access to accounts. The user is also a member of a team in another business unit and the team has a security role that also provides the business-unit-level read access to accounts. Thus, the user is able to read accounts in two business units—the user's own business unit as well as the team's business unit.

How to create a custom security role

There are two methods for creating a custom security role:

- **Create a new security role**: Use this method if you need to specify a few specific entity-based or task-based privileges, or if you need to create a new security role in another business unit
- **Copy an existing security role**: Use this method if you need to create a new job-tailored security role in the same business unit as the existing security role that you want to copy

How to create a new security role

To create a new security role, follow these steps:

1. In the navigation pane, click on **Settings**.
2. In the **System** group, click on **Administration** and then click on **Security Roles**.
3. Click on **New**.

4. Enter the following information:

   ◦ **Role Name**: The security role names must be unique within a business unit. It is best practice to enter a unique name for each security role in your organization.

   ◦ **Business Unit**: The default and best practice is that new security roles are assigned to the root parent business unit.

5. Specify the required security privileges.

6. Click on **Save and Close**.

How to copy an existing security role

Within a business unit, you can make a copy of an existing security role. You cannot make a copy of a security role in a different business unit.

To copy an existing security role, follow these steps:

1. Navigate to the **Security Roles** area.

2. Select the security role that you want to copy.

3. In the **Security Roles** grid toolbar, select **More Actions** and then select **Copy Role...**.

4. In the **Copy Security Role** pop-up window, provide a new role name in the **New Role Name** field.

5. Click on **OK**.

6. Specify the required security privileges.

7. Click on **Save and Close**.

How to use the privilege shortcut

The privilege shortcut feature provides a handy way of quickly updating privileges in a new security role.

To use the privilege shortcut feature, follow these steps:

1. Open a security role.

2. Click on the name of an entity, for example, the **Account** entity, to cycle through the access-levels for that entity.

3. Or, click on the name of a privilege, for example, the **Read** privilege, to cycle through the access-levels for that privilege.

4. Click on **Save and Close**.

Introduction to security privileges

There are two types of security privileges—entity-based security privileges and task-based security privileges.

Entity-based security privileges

The entity-based security privileges define the actions that a user or team can perform on an entity. An entity-based privilege is defined as a combination of an entity action and access level.

Entity actions

The actions that a user can perform on an entity are as follows:

- **Create**: User can create new records of an entity
- **Read**: User can view records of an entity
- **Write**: User can edit or update records of an entity
- **Delete**: User can delete records of an entity
- **Append**: User can associate records of an entity to another record
- **Append To**: User can associate another record to records of an entity
- **Assign**: User can assign records of an entity to another user or team (provided that the other user or team has at least the view privilege for that entity)
- **Share**: User can share records of this entity with another user or team

Often a combination of privileges is required to achieve an action. For example, to add a contact to an account, a user will require the read, write, and append privileges on the contact entity and the append to privilege on the account entity.

Access levels

The access level defines the scope of an entity action. The levels of access that a privilege can have for the user- or team-owned entities, such as the account or contact system entities, are as follows:

- **None**: No access to the privilege on any records
- **User**: Access to the privilege on records that the user owns
- **Business Unit**: Access to the privilege on records owned by any user in the user's business unit

- **Parent: Child Business Units**: Access to the privilege on records owned by any user in the user's business unit or its child business units

- **Organization**: Access to the privilege on records owned by any user in any business unit

Sharing a record with a user who would otherwise not have access to the record, effectively creates an exception to the normal security configuration granted by the security role, security privileges, and access-level combination.

For the organization-owned entities, such as the product or contract template system entities, the only levels of access are as follows:

- **None**: No access to the privilege on any records

- **Organization**: Access to the privilege on records owned by any user in any business unit

Task-based security privileges

The task-based security privileges define the features that a user or team can use.

Examples of task-based privileges are as follows:

- Bulk Delete
- View Audit History
- Create Quick Campaign
- Override Opportunity Pricing
- Publish Articles
- Export to Excel
- Print
- Merge
- Sync to Outlook
- Create Own Calendar
- Execute Workflow Job

The task-based security privileges are either granted or denied. Access levels do not apply to most task-based privileges. Access levels apply to a few task-based privileges, such as the pricing override privileges, in the same way as the entity-based privileges.

Other security features

Microsoft Dynamics CRM 2011 offers a number of other security features that are described in other chapters of this book.

Field security profiles

Field security profiles and field-level security are described in *Chapter 4, Entity and Attribute Customization*. Custom fields on system and custom entities can be configured with the read, create, and update privileges restricted to users or teams who have been assigned a specific field security profile.

Role-based forms

Role-based forms are described in *Chapter 6, User Interface Customization Using Forms, Views, and Charts*. Entity forms can be configured and made available only to users with specific security roles. For example, users with a Customer Service Representative security role might see a different version of the account form compared to users with a Sales Representative security role.

User interface customization

Developers can use the methods described in the Microsoft Dynamics CRM software development kit to display or hide user interface components—such as ribbon buttons, left-hand navigation areas, and form sections—depending upon the user's security role. Such custom development is outside the scope of MB2-866.

Summary

In Microsoft Dynamics CRM 2011, the organization structure is comprised of business units, users, and teams. In this chapter, we learned how to create and manage the organization structure and understood the administration constraints.

We also discussed the different types of client access license available in an on-premise deployment and how these are applied to the CRM user accounts.

Once the organization structure has been configured, we can implement security roles (which define a collection of security privileges) that our users and teams need in order to carry out their work.

Finally, we discussed some of the additional security features — field-level security, role-based forms, and user interface customization — which are described in later chapters.

Now that we've configured our organization structure, it's time to start creating and customizing entities and attributes, which is the subject of our next chapter.

Test your knowledge

Q. 1   Which one of the following options do best describe the components of the security configuration in Microsoft Dynamics CRM 2011?

  1. Business units, users, resource groups, security roles, security privileges

  2. Business units, users, teams, security roles, security privileges

  3. Business units, users, teams, security roles, security privileges, sharing rules

  4. Business units, territories, users, teams, security roles, security privileges

  5. Business units, users, facilities/equipments, teams, security roles, security privileges

Q. 2   Which of the following conditions should be met before a business unit can be deleted (select all that apply)?

  1. It must have no child business units

  2. It must be disabled

  3. Users in the business unit must be disabled

  4. The Undo Delete option must be checked

Q. 3   Which of the following methods can be used to create new CRM users (select all that apply)?

1.   The New User form

2.   The Active Directory synchronization

3.   The New Multiple Users wizard

4.   The Data Import wizard using the Users template

5.   The Clone User wizard

Q. 4   A user's security roles are removed when...

1.   A user's manager is changed

2.   A user is moved to a new business unit

3.   A user is disabled and then re-enabled

4.   A user is assigned to a team in a different business unit

Q. 5   When creating a team the required fields are (select all that apply):

1.   Business Unit

2.   Default Queue

3.   Default Security Role

4.   Administrator

5.   Team Name

4
Entity and Attribute Customization

The customization features of Microsoft Dynamics CRM enable us to modify the database schema so that we can support complex business applications by using a combination of system and custom entities.

In this chapter, we'll discover how we can model our business entities by using the standard customization features that require no programming skills, custom development effort, or direct database access.

In this chapter we shall cover:

- Custom entities
- Custom fields
- Field-level security
- Option sets
- Managing entities in a solution
- Publishing solutions

Custom entities

In this section we will cover:

- Introduction to entities
- Creating custom entities
- Customizing entities

Introduction to entities

In Microsoft Dynamics CRM, an entity represents an object that your organization needs to manage as part of its business processes. For example, if your organization provides insurance, it will need to manage customers, brokers, quotes, policies, and claims (these are examples of entities in an insurance business) as part of its business processes.

Some entities may represent tangible objects such as an insured vehicle, others may represent intangible objects such as a contact's interests.

Microsoft Dynamics CRM 2011 provides hundreds of system entities that are used in marketing, sales, customer support, and service scheduling scenarios. Accounts, contacts, campaigns, opportunities, cases, and service activities are all examples of system entities. You can customize almost all of the system entities and create new custom entities to meet your organization's requirements.

Microsoft Dynamics CRM 2011 takes care of all of the complexity of creating and managing entities so that we can quickly create a new entity. When we create a new entity, the CRM 2011 platform creates:

- Database tables in the SQL Server database for storing records
- A filtered view in the SQL Server database for reporting
- Forms for entering and viewing records
- Views for viewing lists of records
- Security privileges, which can be granted to security roles for controlling user access
- Web service interfaces for programmatic interaction with the entity

Creating custom entities

As we have already learned, the Microsoft Dynamics CRM platform makes it quite easy to create new entities. However, we still need to understand all the options that are available to us while creating a new entity, so that the entity works as we expect and meets our requirements. That's what we'll learn in this section.

You can create custom entities in the default solution, but it is recommended that you create custom entities within a custom solution.

To create a custom entity, follow these steps:

1. In the navigation pane, click on **Settings**.

2. In the **Customization** group, click on **Customization** and then click on **Customize the System** to open the default solution.

3. In the left-hand side navigation area of the solution, click on **Entities**.

4. Click on **New** to open the **New Entity** window.

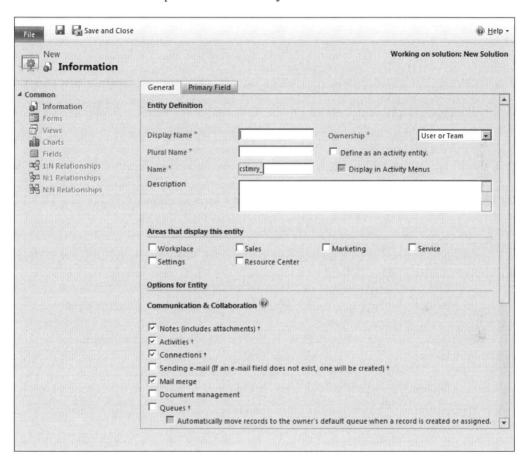

Custom entity options

There are lots of options to consider when creating a custom entity. It's important to know how to choose the right options so that your custom entity meets your requirements. So in this section, we will learn about each option.

Entity definition

The options in this section are as follows:

- **Display Name**: This is the name of the entity your users will see. It can be changed later.

- **Plural Name**: This is the plural name of the entity your users will see. It can be changed later.

- **Name**: This is the schema name of the entity that your developers will use. It cannot be changed later. This name is prefixed with the customization prefix set by the publisher of the entity's solution. This name is used as the table name in the SQL Server database.

- **Ownership**: This field determines whether records of this entity will be owned by a user or a team or by an organization. The records owned by a user or a team can be assigned to a user or team whereas the records owned by an organization cannot be owned by anyone. You can apply the security privileges at the user, business unit, parent-child business unit, or organization level to the user- or team-owned entities, but the security privileges at the organization level can be applied only to the organization-owned entities. This option cannot be changed later, so it is important to consider your security requirements carefully before creating a new entity.

- **Define as an activity entity**: This field determines whether your custom entity will be a custom activity entity. Activity entities—such as task, appointment, and e-mail—have special properties. For example, they can be associated with many other entities using the **Set Regarding** field and they can make use of the **Activity Party** field to be associated with multiple accounts, leads, or contacts in a single field. However, you cannot apply security privileges to the custom activity entities (activity security privileges apply to all types of activities) and you cannot synchronize custom activity entities with Outlook.

- **Display in Activity Menus**: This checkbox determines whether the entity will be displayed in activity menus or not.

Areas that display the entity

The options in this section represent the high-level navigation groups (defined in the SiteMap). The standard areas are Workplace, Sales, Marketing, Service, Settings, Resource Center. If you have customized the SiteMap, the navigation group options may vary.

Selecting an option causes your custom entity to be available in the corresponding navigation group.

Communications and collaboration

The options in this section are as follows:

- **Notes (includes attachments)**: This option enables notes and attachments for your custom entity. Once you enable this option, it cannot be disabled.

- **Activities**: This option enables the activities for your custom entities so that activity records can be associated with this entity. If this option is enabled, the **Activities** and **Closed Activities** navigation links are added to the entity forms. Once you enable this option, it cannot be disabled.

- **Connections**: This option enables connections for your custom entity so that you can create connections between this entity's records and other records. If this option is enabled, a **Connections** navigation link is added to the entity forms. Once you enable this option, it cannot be disabled.

- **Sending e-mail**: This option enables direct e-mail messages to be sent to the records of this entity from the entity's grid screen. Unless there is already an e-mail field, a new e-mail field called **E-mail Address** will be created. Once you enable this option, it cannot be disabled.

- **Mail merge**: This option enables the mail merge feature for records of the entity.

- **Document management**: This option enables the SharePoint-integrated document management feature for this entity.

- **Queues**: This option enables the records of this entity to be added to a queue to help you manage workloads.

- **Automatically move records to the owner's default queue when a record is created or assigned**: Every user and team has a default queue. Selecting this option will cause all records assigned to the user or team to appear in the user's or team's default queue.

Best practice — do not select default options

Several options in this section — Notes, Activities, Connections, Sending e-mail, and Queues — cannot be disabled after you have enabled them and by default the checkboxes for Notes, Activities, and Connections are enabled (checked). It is good practice to disable (uncheck) these options while creating the entity and to enable them later only when you have confirmed the requirement to enable these options.

How do you remember which options can't be disabled later?

Never Allow Customization So Quickly!

Notes, **Activities**, **Connections**, **Sending e-mail**, and **Queues**.

Data services

The options in this section are as follows:

- **Duplicate detection**: This option enables duplicate detection for the entity. The duplicate detection rules can only be defined for the duplicate detection-enabled entities.
- **Auditing**: This option enables changes to this entity's records to be audited. The global auditing settings must be configured before entity-level auditing starts.

Outlook and mobile

The options in this section are as follows:

- **Mobile Express**: Displays the entity in the Mobile Express web client.
- **Reading pane in CRM for Outlook**: Enables the Outlook reading pane option in the CRM for Outlook client.
- **Offline access in CRM for Outlook**: Enables users to work with records of the entity when using the CRM for Outlook with the Offline Access client.

Custom entity privileges

After you create a new custom entity, a new set of privileges will appear in the **Custom Entities** tab of all the security role forms so that you can specify how users can work with your custom entity.

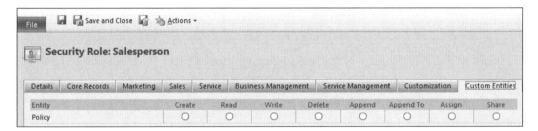

Your users will not be able to work with your custom entity until you configure the privileges for your users' security roles.

Custom activities are the exception to this requirement. There are no separate security privileges for custom activity entities, they are included in the security privileges for the activity entity, which is configured under the **Core Records** tab in the security role form.

Customizing entities

In the previous section, we learned how to create new custom entities. In this section, we will examine the additional customizations that we can make to custom and system entities:

- Customizing an entity from a grid or form
- Showing an entity's dependencies
- Publishing an entity
- Updating an entity's icons
- Deleting an entity
- Reviewing an entity's managed properties

Customizing an entity from a grid or form

You can customize an entity by opening a solution and selecting the entity that you want to customize.

There are two additional methods for customizing an entity—from a grid or from a form. However, these methods will customize the entity in your default solution. If you want to customize the entity in another solution, open the appropriate solution and select the entity that you want to customize.

Customizing an entity from a grid

To customize an entity from a grid, follow these steps:

1. Navigate to the entity's grid screen.
2. Under the **Customize** tab of the entity ribbon, click on **Customize Entity**. This will open the **Entity** form in the default solution.

Customizing an entity from a form

To customize an entity from a form, follow these steps:

1. Open a record for the entity.

2. Under the **Customize** tab of the form ribbon, click on **Customize Entity**. This will open the entity form in the default solution.

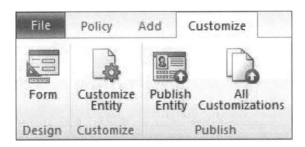

Showing an entity's dependencies

The **Show Dependencies** button displays the solution component dependencies for the currently selected entity.

To show dependencies for an entity, follow these steps:

1. In the navigation pane, click on **Settings**.

2. In the **Customization** group, click on **Customizations** and then click on **Customize the System** to open the default solution.

3. Expand the **Entities** component and expand the entity that you want to examine.

4. In the **Solution** toolbar, click on **Show Dependencies**.

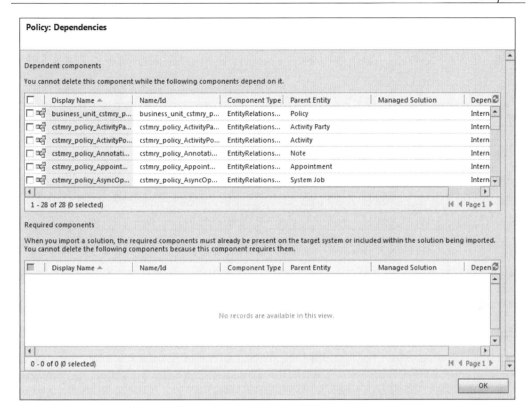

The **Dependent components** section shows the solution components, such as entity relationships, which depend upon your entity. If you delete your entity, these dependent components will also be deleted.

Publishing an entity

The **Publish** button publishes the changes to the currently selected entity. For example, form and view customizations must be published before the changes you have made are visible to your users.

To publish customizations that you have made to an entity, follow these steps:

1. In the navigation pane, click on **Settings**.
2. In the **Customization** group, click on **Customizations** and then click on **Customize the System** to open the default solution.
3. Expand the **Entities** component.
4. In the components grid, select the entity that you want to publish and click on the **Publish** button.

Updating the entity's icons

Microsoft Dynamics CRM uses the same custom entity icons for all custom entities. To make it easier for your users to distinguish custom entities, the icons associated with an entity can be changed.

There are two icons that are used in Microsoft Dynamics CRM 2011:

- **16 px x 16 px icon in web application**:
    - ○ gif, png, or jpg file format
    - ○ Displayed in grids and shortcuts
    - ○ Must be less than 10 KB

- **32 px x 32 px icon for forms**:
    - ○ 16 colors
    - ○ gif, png, or jpg file format
    - ○ Displayed in forms
    - ○ Must be less than 10 KB

The Microsoft official courseware for Microsoft Dynamics CRM 2011 refers to a third icon (66 px x 48 px) as the icon for the entity forms, and refers to the 32 px x 32 px icon as the shortcut icon for Microsoft Dynamics CRM for Outlook. This information is incorrect due to some late changes to Microsoft Dynamics CRM 2011. Exam questions regarding icon sizes are unlikely, but be careful because the correct answer may be based on the incorrect information provided in the official courseware.

How to update the entity icons

To update the entity icons for a custom entity, you need to prepare two graphic files and upload them as web resources in your solution before associating the icons with your entity.

To upload icons as web resources, follow these steps:

1. In the navigation pane, click on **Settings**.
2. In the **Customization** group, click on **Customizations** and then click on **Customize the System** to open the default solution.
3. In the left-hand side navigation, click on **Web Resources**.
4. Click on **New**.

5. Provide a name in the **Name** field, and optionally, fill in the **Display Name** and **Description** fields.

6. Specify the **Type**. This should be **JPG format**, **GIF format**, or **PNG format**.

7. Click on **Browse** and upload the graphic file from your computer.

8. Click on **Save and Close**.

To update the icons for an entity, follow these steps:

1. In the navigation pane, click on **Settings**.

2. In the **Customization** group, click on **Customizations** and then click on **Customize the System** to open the default solution.

3. Expand the **Entities** component and open the entity that you want to customize.

4. Click on **Update Icons**.

5. In the **Select New Icons** pop-up window, select the web resources that you have previously uploaded for the 16 px x 16 px and 32 px x 32 px icons (a 66 px x 48 px icon is not required).

6. Click on **OK**.

Although the icon changes do not need to be published to take effect, icons can be cached by the server or by the client. So it may take some time for the icon changes to be seen by your users.

Delete

You can delete a custom entity, but system entities cannot be deleted.

Warning

Deleting a custom entity deletes all records of that entity. Associated records, such as notes, may also be deleted depending on the **Cascade Delete** property of the entity relationships. Ensure that you no longer need the data before deleting an entity.

Deleting a custom entity

To delete a custom entity, follow these steps:

1. In the navigation pane, click on **Settings**.

2. In the **Customization** group, click on **Customizations** and click on **Customize the System** to open the default solution.

3. Click on the **Entities** component and select the entity that you want to delete.

4. In the solution toolbar, click on **Delete**.

5. Click on **OK** to confirm if you want to delete the entity and all its records.

Managed properties

If you export your solution as a managed solution, the **Managed Properties** options enable you to control whether or not some properties of your entity can be modified after the managed solution has been imported into another organization.

Refer to *Chapter 8*, *Solutions* for more information about solutions and managed properties.

Custom fields

Almost all implementations of Microsoft Dynamics CRM involve customized fields. Even the out-of-the-box implementations, where the objective is to avoid customization and custom development by using only standard features, often involve renaming some entities, fields, and option set values.

Microsoft Dynamics CRM 2011 provides web-based, graphical features for field customization so that most business requirements can be achieved without any specialist programming skills.

In this section we will discuss:

- Introduction to fields
- Field datatypes
- Field properties
- Customizing fields
- Creating custom fields
- Modifying existing fields

Introduction to fields

In Microsoft Dynamics CRM, a **field** (also known as an **attribute**) represents a characteristic of an entity that your organization needs to manage as part of its business process.

For example, if your organization provides insurance, it will need to manage information about its insurance policies—policy number, start date, end date, premium amount, insured value, and insured customer (these are examples of fields of an insurance policy in an insurance business).

Microsoft Dynamics CRM 2011 provides hundreds of system fields in the system entities that are used in marketing, sales, customer support, and service scheduling scenarios. You can customize almost all of the system fields and create new custom fields to meet your organization's requirements. System fields cannot be deleted, although most can be modified—your custom fields can be modified and deleted.

Microsoft Dynamics CRM 2011 takes care of all of the complexity of creating and managing fields so that we can quickly create a new field and use it in the system. When we create a new entity, the CRM 2011 platform performs the following tasks:

- Creates a database column in the SQL Server database table for storing field values
- Adds the column to the filtered view in the SQL Server database for reporting
- Makes the field available for you to add it to the forms, views, charts, and reports
- Makes the field available to web service interfaces for programmatic interaction

Field datatypes

In Microsoft Dynamics CRM, every field has a datatype property, which specifies the type of information that will be stored in the field. The datatype cannot be changed, so it is an important consideration to make when customizing your system.

The datatypes available in Microsoft Dynamics CRM 2011 and the corresponding SQL Server datatypes are shown in the following table:

CRM datatype	SQL Server datatype
Single line of text	Nvarchar
Option set	Int
Two options	Bit
Whole number	Int
Floating point number	Float
Decimal number	Decimal
Currency	Money

CRM datatype	SQL Server datatype
Multiple lines of text	nvarchar(max)
Date and time	Datetime
Lookup	Uniqueidentifier

Datatype descriptions

The following section provides a brief description of each of the datatypes.

Single line of text

A single line of text field is used to store a specified number of text characters — the maximum number of characters is 4,000. Text fields are stored in the unicode format, which requires two bytes of storage per character.

There are several format options available for the single line of text fields:

- **Text**: This will display a single line of text.
- **E-mail**: This will display a hyperlink. Double-clicking on the field value will open up a new e-mail form in the user's default e-mail client. Text entered into the field is validated to ensure that it represents a valid e-mail address.
- **Text-area**: This will display a configurable number of lines of text with a vertical scroll bar.
- **URL**: This will display a hyperlink. Double-clicking on the field value will open a new browser window pointed at the URL address. Text entered into the field is validated to ensure that it represents a valid URL.
- **Ticker symbol**: This will display a hyperlink. Double-clicking on the field value will open a new browser window pointed at **MSN Money** and use the field value to search for a stock.

Option set

An **option set** field (also known as a **picklist** or **drop-down list**) is used to store a specific option from within a constrained set of options.

Refer to the *Option sets* section discussed later in this chapter for more information about creating and managing option sets.

Two options

A **two options** field (also known as a **bit field**, **checkbox**, or **radio button**) is used to store one of two possible options. In the database, these options are represented by 1 and 0. However, for each two option field the options can be labeled according to your requirements, for example, Hot and Cold, True and False, or Yes and No.

One of the two options must be specified as the default option and it will be used when new records are created.

When this field is added to a form, you can specify whether the two option fields should be displayed as a picklist, checkbox, or radio button. Each of these display types has its own advantages depending on your scenario. The display type can be modified as required.

Whole number

A **whole number** field is used to store a positive or negative number without any decimal places. You can specify the minimum and maximum permitted values between- 2,147,483,648 and 2,147,483,647.

The whole number fields cannot have leading zeroes and are displayed with a user-specified thousands separator. This makes them unsuitable for some uses, such as a numeric record identifier, where a single line of text field might be more appropriate.

In addition to the general whole number field format, there are three special types of whole number field formats:

- **Duration**: This format displays a picklist of duration increments between 1 minute and 3 days. The value stored in the database is the duration in minutes.

- **Time zone**: This format displays a picklist of time zones and time zone names. The value stored in the database is a code representing the time zone (the time zone code definitions are stored in a separate table in the database).

- **Language**: This format displays a picklist of all the languages installed in the organization. The value stored in the database is the language code.

Floating point number

A **floating point number** field is used to store a positive or negative number with a precision of up to five decimal places. You can specify the minimum and maximum permitted values between- 1,000,000,000 and 1,000,000,000.

Decimal number

A **decimal number** field, like a floating point number field, is used to store a positive or negative number, but decimal number fields can have a precision up to 10 decimal places. You can specify the minimum and maximum permitted values between-1,000,000,000 and 1,000,000,000.

Floating point or decimal number

Floating point numbers and decimal numbers are very similar. There are differences in how they are stored in SQL Server (decimal number values consume more storage) and the precision of results using each type in calculations (decimal numbers are more accurate but calculations can take longer). If you plan on synchronizing the data in a number field, it is best to use the same datatype as the corresponding field in your target system.

Currency

A **currency** field is used to store a monetary value with a precision of up to four decimal places. The precision for a currency field can be set to inherit the pricing decimal precision value from the system settings, inherit the currency precision specified for each currency, or set to a value between 0 and 4.

You can specify the minimum and maximum permitted values between-922,337,203,685,477 and 922,337,203,685,477.

When you create the first currency field on an entity, the following four fields are created:

- Your custom currency field to store the monetary value
- A currency field to store the currency code
- An exchange rate field to store the exchange rate between the record currency and the system currency at the point of time when the field is updated
- Your custom currency field in the base system currency

For subsequent currency fields, only the custom currency field and the base currency field are created.

Multiple lines of text

A **multiple lines of text** field is used to store configurable amounts of text, up to 100,000 characters.

When this field is added to a form, you can specify how many lines the textbox will use or expand the field to fill all the available space on the form.

Date and time

A **date and time** field is used to store a date and time, from midnight January 1, 1900 in the UTC format plus or minus the user's UTC time zone offset.

There are two types of the date and time field formats:

- **Date only**: This format displays only the date and provides a calendar date control when it is added to a form.
- **Date and time**: This format displays the date and time, and provides both a calendar date control and time control when this format is added to a form.

The **Personal Options** settings can be used to set a user's current time zone as well as date and time display preferences.

Lookup

A **lookup** field is used to store the globally unique identifier of another CRM record.

Creating a lookup field is a quick method for creating a many-to-one relationship between your entity and a target entity. You only need to specify the target entity and a relationship name.

Additional properties regarding the custom relationship can be managed in the entity's N:1 Relationships area. For more information on managing entity relationships, see *Chapter 5, Data Modeling Using Entity Relationships*.

Field properties

All fields have a number of properties. You can modify the properties of custom fields to meet your requirements, while the properties of the system fields may be constrained.

The field properties that can be modified are as follows:

- **Display Name**
- **Name**
- **Requirement Level**
- **Searchable**
- **Field Security**
- **Auditing**

- **Description**
- **IME Mode**

General		
Schema		
Display Name *	Name	Requirement Level * Business Required
Name *	cstmry_name	Searchable Yes
Field Security	○ Enable ● Disable	
Auditing *	● Enable ○ Disable	
	⚠ This field will not be audited until you enable auditing on the entity.	
Description	The name of the custom entity.	
For information about how to interact with entities and fields programmatically, see the Microsoft Dynamics CRM SDK		

Display Name

Display Name for a field is the label shown in the user interface in forms, views, charts, and reports (although the form label can be modified). The display name can be up to 50 characters, and can be modified after the field is created.

Name

Name for a field is the schema or system name that is used to refer to a unique field. The name can be between 1 to 41 alpha-numeric characters (up to nine characters are reserved for the prefix). The name cannot be modified once the field is created — for system fields, the name cannot be modified at all. The field's schema name is also the column name in the underlying SQL Server database.

Requirement Level

Requirement Level determines whether or not the user must enter a value into this field when creating or modifying a record through the user interface. There are three possible values for this field:

- **No Constraint**: Entering a value is optional
- **Business Recommended**: Entering a value is recommended but not mandatory
- **Business Required**: Entering a value is required and the system will warn the user and prevent the user from saving the record until a value is entered

The requirement level is not a constraint when records are created through other methods, for example, when records are imported or created programmatically.

If a field's requirement level is modified to **Business Required**, the user must enter a value in the field when updating any existing records.

System Required

There is a special requirement level, **System Required**, reserved for some system fields which you cannot set for system or custom fields. Records cannot be imported or created programmatically unless they have a value for the **System Required** field. For example, the **Potential Customer** field on the opportunity entity has a requirement level of **System Required**, so an opportunity record cannot be created programmatically unless a potential customer is specified.

Searchable

The **Searchable** property determines whether users can use the field within an **Advanced Find** query. By default, most system fields and all custom fields are searchable. It can be useful to set the **Searchable** property to **No** for the fields that do not need to be queried.

Field Security

The **Field Security** property determines whether access to the field can be restricted through a field-level security profile or not. Only custom fields with the **Field Security** property of **Enabled** can be restricted through a field-level security profile. **Field Security** for the system fields cannot be enabled.

See the *Field-level Security* section discussed later in this chapter for more information about working with secured fields and field security profiles.

Auditing

The **Auditing** property determines whether modifications to the field are audited or not (if the system-level auditing and the entity-level auditing are also enabled).

Refer to *Chapter 7, Auditing* for more information about configuring the auditing options.

Description

The **Description** property provides a definition of the field that is useful to other customizers. It is good practice to enter a description for all fields before deploying a new system to production and to periodically review the descriptions for all fields that are currently in use.

IME mode

The **Input Method Editing** (**IME**) mode makes it easier to input the Chinese, Korean, and Japanese characters that do not normally appear in the Roman character sets on the Western keyboards.

There are four options available for **IME Mode**:

- **Auto**: IME mode not affected.
- **Active**: All characters are entered in the IME mode, but you can still deactivate it.
- **Inactive**: All characters are entered without using the IME mode, but you can still activate it.
- **Disabled**: All characters are entered without using the IME mode and you cannot activate it.

Customizing fields

If Microsoft Dynamics CRM does not have an existing field that meets your requirements, there are two options available to you:

- Create a custom field that meets your requirements
- Modify an unused system field to meet your requirements

Before customizing your system, it is worth weighing up the advantages and disadvantages of each option for your scenario given by your business requirements.

Advantages of creating a custom field

There are several advantages to creating a custom field:

- You are not restricted by any constraints on system fields. For example, the field-level security cannot be applied to the system fields, so if you think you might need the field-level security applied to your field (now or in the future) a custom field is advantageous.

- You do not need to be concerned with where the system field might already be used in the system. For example, some system fields are displayed in forms, views, charts, and reports that may not be required in your scenario and you may need to spend time in removing the field from forms, views, charts, and reports, where it is not needed.

- You do not need to be concerned that the system field may be needed in future.

Advantages of modifying a system field

There are several advantages to modifying an unused system field:

- Your requirement may already be met by a system field that has a different name. For example, if you have a requirement for an **Account Manager** field on the account entity, it may be better to re-use and rename the existing **Owner** field rather than create a new field.

- Using a system field needs less storage. The Microsoft SQL Server limitations restrict Microsoft Dynamics CRM to 1,023 custom fields per entity and 8,060 bytes per row. Using system fields, makes it less likely that you will be impacted by the database limitations.

Modifying the existing fields

Most of the properties of the system and custom fields can be modified after the field has been created. It is worth reminding ourselves that there are several important properties that cannot be modified.

The field properties that cannot be modified are as follows:

- **Name**: The display name can be modified but the schema name cannot.

- **Datatype**: If you need to change the datatype that you will need for deleting the field and creating a new field with the appropriate datatype.

- **Format**: The format cannot be modified for most datatypes, however, the format of the date and time fields can be modified.

- **Field security**: This can be applied to the custom fields, but cannot be applied to the system fields.

Creating custom fields

Microsoft Dynamics CRM 2011 provides a user interface that enables customizers to create custom fields easily.

To create a custom field, perform the following steps:

1. In the navigation pane, click on **Settings**.

2. In the **Customization** group, click on **Customizations**, and then click on **Customize the System** to open the default solution.

3. Expand the **Entities** component and expand the entity that you want to customize.

4. Click on the **Fields** sub-component and then click on **New**.

5. Specify the field properties according to your requirements.

6. Click on **Save and Close**.

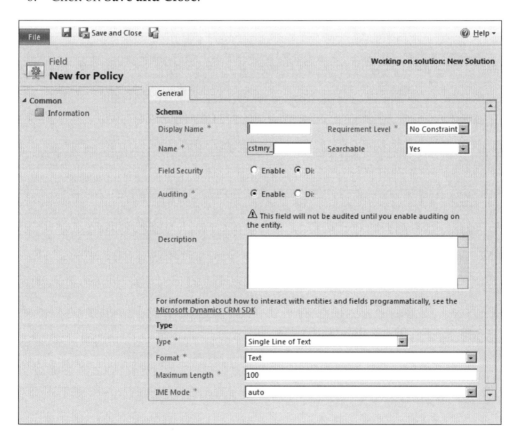

Once the field has been saved, it is available to:

- Users through Advanced Find, Report Wizard, Export to Excel, user views, and charts
- The CRM SDK

However, the field will not appear on a form or a system view until you add the field to a form or system view, and publish the entity.

Field-level security

Field-level security is a new feature in Microsoft Dynamics CRM 2011 that enables you to control access to custom fields. Field-level security is not supported for system fields.

Once the field-level security has been applied to a field, users are unable to work with the field unless they have the appropriate field security profile. A field security profile defines the read, update, and create permissions for a collection of secure fields.

> Imagine you have a requirement to store the Government ID for a contact, but this sensitive data should only be available to users who have passed a background check. Using the field-level security, we can create a custom field (the field-level security cannot be applied to the Government ID system field on the contact entity), we can define a field-level security profile that will enable users to read and update the custom field, and apply the field security profile to a team of users that have passed their background checks.

The field-level security is comprehensive. Unless the users have a field security profile providing the appropriate permissions (or a System Administrator security role), users cannot work with secure fields in the forms, views, charts, Advanced Find, Export to Excel, Report Wizard, offline access, duplicate detection, workflows, or CRM SDK.

In this section we will learn about:

- Enabling field-level security
- Creating a field security profile
- Applying a field security profile

Enabling field-level security

Field-level security can be enabled for any custom field:

To enable the field-level security, follow these steps:

1. In the navigation pane, click on **Settings**.

2. In the **Customization** group, click on **Customizations** and then click on **Customize the System** to open the default solution.

3. Expand the **Entities** component and expand the entity that you want to customize.

4. Click on the **Fields** sub-component and open the field that you want to customize.

5. In the field's **Field Security** property, select **Enable**.

6. Then click on **Save and Close** to close the field form.

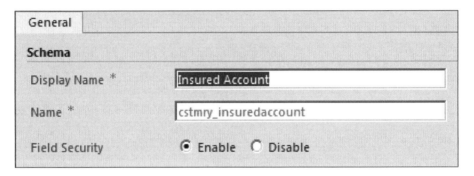

Secure fields appear in the form designer with a key icon indicating that field security has been enabled.

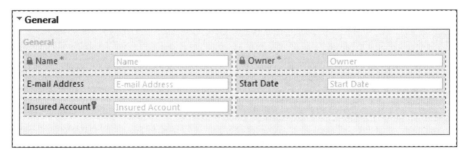

Creating a field security profile

Once security for a field has been enabled, it can be added to a field security profile so that we can specify the read, update, and create permissions granted to users or teams.

To create a field security profile, follow these steps:

1. In the navigation pane, click on **Settings**.
2. In the **Customization** group, click on **Customizations** and then click on **Customize the System** to open the default solution.
3. Click on the **Field Security Profiles** component and then click on **New**.
4. Provide a name for the field security profile and, optionally a **Description**.
5. Click on **Save**.
6. Click on **Field Permissions** to display a grid of all the secure fields in the solution.
7. Select the field that you want to modify and click on **Edit**.
8. In the **Edit Field Security** pop-up window, specify the permissions that you want to grant to this field security profile. You can select from **Allow Read**, **Allow Update**, and **Allow Create**.
9. Click on **OK**.
10. Click on **Save and Close**.

Applying a field security profile

After you have created the field security profiles according to your security requirements, you need to apply the field-level security profiles to the appropriate users or teams.

To apply a field security profile to a user or team, follow these steps:

1. In the navigation pane, click on **Settings**.

2. In the **Customization** group, click on **Customizations** and then click on **Customize the System** to open the default solution.

3. Click on the **Field Security Profiles** component and open the field security profile that you want to apply to a users or team.

4. To apply the field security profile to a team, click on **Teams**, then click on **Add**, find the appropriate team in the **Lookup Records** window, and then click on **OK**.

5. To apply the field security profile to a user, click on Users, then click on **Add**, find the appropriate user in the **Lookup Records** window, and then click on **OK**.

6. Click on **Save and Close**.

Option sets

An **option set** is a field with a constrained set of options from which users can choose one value. An option set field is sometimes called a **picklist** or **dropdown** field.

In previous versions of Microsoft Dynamics CRM, option sets could not be re-used and had to be redefined separately each time you wanted the same field with the same options to be used on different entities.

Using the new global option sets feature in Microsoft Dynamics CRM 2011, you can define an option set once and re-use it in multiple entities or even for the multiple times within the same entity. When you update the options for a global option set, all fields that reference the global option set are updated. This makes option set maintenance much easier for the system administrators and makes option sets easier to use for users and developers.

In this section we'll learn about:

- Creating a global option set
- Modifying a global option set
- Deleting a global option set

Creating a global option set

There are two methods for creating a global option set:

- **Method 1**: Using this method, you will create a global option set first, and then create one or more fields associated with the global option set
- **Method 2**: Using this method, you will create the global option set while you create the field

Method 1: Creating the global option set first

To create the global option set, follow these steps:

1. In the navigation pane, click on **Settings**.
2. In the **Customization** group, click on **Customizations** and then click on **Customize the System** to open the default solution.
3. Click on the **Global Option Sets** component and then click on **New**.
4. Provide a display name in the **Display Name** field.
5. In the **Options** section, click on the **Add** icon (a green plus sign) to add a new option and provide a label for the option in the **Label** field.
6. Continue to add options, you will meet your requirements.
7. Once you have finished with adding the options, click on **Save and Close**.

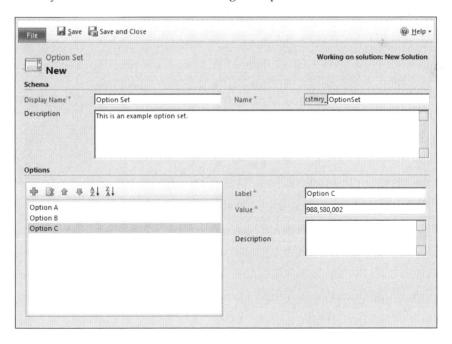

Once you have created a global option set, it can be used when you create a new option set field in any entity in the solution in which you have created the global option set.

To create a new option set field associated with a global option set, follow these steps:

1. In the navigation pane, click on **Settings**.

2. In the **Customization** group, click on **Customizations** and then click on **Customize the System** to open the default solution.

3. Expand the **Entities** component and then expand the appropriate entity.

4. Click on the **Fields** section and then click on **New**.

5. In the new **Field** form:

   a. Provide a display name.

   b. Specify **Type** as **Option Set**.

   c. Set **Use Existing Option Set** to **Yes**.

   d. Set the **Option Set** value to your custom global option set.

   e. Optionally, specify a default value.

6. Click on **Save and Close**.

Method 2: Creating the global option set while creating the field

To create the field, follow these steps:

1. In the navigation pane, click on **Settings**.

2. In the **Customization** group, click on **Customizations** and then click on **Customize the System** to open the default solution.

3. Expand the **Entities** component and then expand the appropriate entity.

4. Click on the **Fields** section and then click on **New**.

5. In the new **Field** form:

   a. Provide a display name in the **Display Name** field.

   b. Specify the **Type** as **Option Set**.

c.   Next to **Use Existing Option Set**, click on **New**.

d.   In the **New Global Option Set** pop-up window, provide a
     display name.

e.   In the **Options** section, click on the **Add** icon (a green plus sign)
     to add a new option and provide a label for the option in the
     Lable field.

f.   Continue to add options to meet your requirements.

g.   Once you have finished with adding the options, click on **Save and
     Close** to close the **New Global Option Set** pop-up window.

6.   Click on **Save and Close**.

Modifying a global option set

You can modify a global option set any time after creating it. The modifications will
appear in all option set fields associated with your global option set.

To modify a global option set, follow these steps:

1.   In the navigation pane, click on **Settings**.

2.   In the **Customization** group, click on **Customizations** and then click on
     Customize the System to open the default solution.

3.   Click on the **Global Option Sets** component and open the global option set
     that you want to modify.

4.   Modify the required properties of your global option set. The following
     properties can be modified:

     ◦   **Display Name** and **Description**

     ◦   **Option Value Names**, **Sort Order**, and **Descriptions**

     ◦   **Create New Option Set Values** and **Delete Existing Values**

5.   Click on **Save** to save your changes.

6.   Click on **Publish** to publish your changes. This will affect all the option set
     fields associated with your global option set.

Deleting a global option set

You can delete only global option sets that are not currently associated with an option set field. If an option set field is currently associated with a global option set that you want to delete, first you will need to delete the option set field or associate it with a different global option set.

To delete a global option set, follow these steps:

1. In the navigation pane, click on **Settings**.

2. In the **Customization** group, click on **Customizations** and then click on **Customize the System** to open the default solution.

3. Click on the **Global Option Sets** component.

4. Select the global option set that you want to delete and then click on the **Delete** button.

5. Click on **OK** to confirm deletion.

Managing entities in a solution

In this section, we'll learn how to include an existing entity in our solution. Refer to *Chapter 8, Solutions* for more detailed explanations about how to use solutions.

Adding an existing entity to a solution

Within a solution you can customize an entity that was created in another solution by including a reference to that entity from within your solution.

Imagine you have a requirement to add some new fields and a view to a custom entity called Policy. The Policy entity belongs to a managed solution called Insurance Works 1.0.0.0, which was imported into your CRM organization.

To modify the Policy entity, we first create our own solution and then add the existing Policy entity to it so that we can modify it.

To add an existing entity to a solution, follow these steps:

1. In the navigation pane, click on **Settings**.

2. In the **Customization** group, click on **Customizations** and then click on **Customize the System** to open the default solution.

3. Click on the **Entities** component and in the entities grid toolbar, click on **Add Existing**.

4. In the **Select Solution Components** pop-up window, browse through the available entities and then check the entity that you want to add to your solution and click on **OK**.

5. The **Missing Required Components** pop-up window will appear if the entity is dependent on other solution components. Select **Yes** and include required components, or select **No** and do not include required components, and then click on **OK**. You need to include only the required components, if you want to customize those components too.

When you add an existing entity to your solution, you are, in fact, only adding a reference to the entity to your solution. The original definition of the entity remains in the original solution—either the default solution or a managed solution.

Removing an existing entity from a solution

When you remove an existing entity from a solution, you actually remove the reference to the entity. The entity itself still exists, either in the default solution or a managed solution.

To remove an existing entity from a solution, follow these steps:

1. In the navigation pane, click on **Settings**.

2. In the **Customization** group, click on **Customizations** and then click on **Customize the System** to open the default solution.

3. Click on the **Entities** component and in the entities grid toolbar, click on **Remove**.

The entity will be removed from your solution without any confirmation or warning.

Publishing solutions

Earlier in this chapter, we learned how to publish the changes that we make to an entity. We can also publish all the customizations in our organization to ensure that all the recent changes we have made are available to our users.

To publish all customizations, follow these steps:

1. In the navigation pane, click on **Settings**.
2. In the **Customization** group, click on **Solutions**.
3. In the solutions grid toolbar, click on **Publish All Customizations**.

The **Publish All Customizations** feature publishes all customizations in all solutions regardless of which solutions you may have selected in the solutions grid.

Summary

Here's a brief recap of what we've learned in this chapter.

In Microsoft Dynamics CRM, an entity represents a tangible or intangible object that your organization needs to manage as part of its business processes.

You can customize the entities from within a solution, but sometimes it is more convenient to customize an entity from within the entity grid screen or entity form. When we create custom entities, there are some options that cannot be modified later, so it's important to know what each entity option does when we create the custom entities.

After modifying an entity, the changes need to be published. You can publish the customizations for a single entity, or publish all customizations for all entities in all solutions.

You can change the icons associated with the system and custom entities. Two icons are required—a 16 px x 16 px icon and a 32 px x 32 px icon.

Custom entities can be deleted. This also deletes all the records of the custom entity and may also delete associated records, depending on the **Cascade Delete** properties of the entity relationships. System entities cannot be deleted.

In Microsoft Dynamics CRM, a field (also known as an attribute) represents a characteristic of an entity that your organization needs to manage as part of its business process.

When you create a field, you will need to specify a datatype. Fields also have a number of configurable properties. The MB2-866 exam will expect us to know about each of the field datatypes and properties, including which properties can be modified after the field has been created.

Once a field is created, it is immediately available to users—through Advanced Find, Report Wizard, Export to Excel, user views, and charts, and also available through the CRM SDK—without being published. However, the field will not appear on a form or a system view until it has been added to the form or view and the entity has been published.

The field-level security can be applied to the custom fields, but not to the system fields. Users are unable to work with the secure fields unless they have been granted permissions through a field security profile. Field security profiles define a collection of permissions for the secure fields that can be applied to users and/or teams.

An option set is a field with a constrained set of options from which users can choose one value. A global option set is an option set that can be associated with the option set fields so that the options can be easily modified.

Test your knowledge

Q. 1   Which of the following procedures should be followed after creating a custom entity?

1. Create system views for active and inactive records of the custom entity

2. Configure privileges on security profiles so that users can work with records of the custom entity

3. Deploy a web service to enable programmatic interaction with the entity

4. Create filtered views in SQL Server for reporting on records of the custom entity

Q. 2   Which of the following entity options can be modified after an entity has been created? (choose two of the following options)

1. Define as an Activity Entity

2. Display Name

3. Name

4. Ownership

5. Plural Name

Q. 3   Which of the following datatypes exist in Microsoft Dynamics CRM 2011 (choose all the correct options) ?

1. Floating Point number

2. Calculated number

3. Decimal number

4. Option set

5. Multiple option set

Q. 4   Which of the following field properties cannot be modified after a field has been created?

1. Datatype

2. Format of date and time fields

3. Field-level security of custom fields

4. Name

5. Requirement level

Q.5   Which of the following field-level permissions are managed using a field security profile (choose the two correct options)?

1. Read

2. Query

3. Update

4. Null

5. Delete

5
Data Modeling Using Entity Relationships

This chapter explains the concepts and techniques required to establish relationships and mappings between entities. In this chapter, you will learn about the different types of supported entity relationships to meet your data modeling requirements and how to use entity mappings to reduce the data entry required when new child records are created. We'll also see how connections can be used to model relationships between any two records. A self-test section at the end of the chapter will test your knowledge.

In this chapter we will learn about:

- Entity relationships
- Mappings
- Connections

Introduction to entity relationships

To manage your organization's processes in Microsoft Dynamics CRM, you'll need to create relationships between the entities it manages during those processes.

Using Microsoft Dynamics CRM 2011, you can create two different types of supported entity relationships.

In this section we'll learn about:

- Types of entity relationships
- Unsupported relationship types
- 1:N relationships
- N:N relationships
- Self-referential relationships

Types of entity relationships

Using the customization features of Microsoft Dynamics CRM 2011, we can define two different types of entity relationships:

- **1:N (one-to-many)**: For example, a customer can have many opportunities, and an opportunity can be associated with one customer

- **N:N (many-to-many)**: For example, a contact can be a member of many marketing lists, and marketing lists can have many contacts as members

Unsupported relationship types

There are two types of entity relationships that are not supported by Microsoft Dynamics CRM 2011:

- **1:1 (one-to-one)**: These types of relationships are useful in scenarios where one type of record becomes another type of record, for example, where a prospect becomes a customer or a student becomes a graduate. In Microsoft Dynamics CRM 2011, there are a limited number of standard 1:1 relationships—for example, a lead can become an account and a queue item is associated with one case or activity record. You cannot create custom 1:1 relationships without custom development.

- **Polymorphic relationships**: These types of relationships are useful when the primary record in a relationship could be one of several different entity types. For example, a customer complaint could be about a case, invoice, or order. In Microsoft Dynamics CRM 2011, there are one or two standard polymorphic relationships—for example, the customer of an opportunity can be an account or a contact, and the regarding record of an activity can be one of many different entities. You cannot create a custom polymorphic relationship.

1:N relationships

In a 1:N relationship, a primary record can be associated with zero or more related records, and the related records can be associated with one primary record.

N:1 relationships

We create a custom 1:N relationship in Microsoft Dynamics CRM 2011 from the primary entity by specifying the related entity type. We can also create a custom N:1 relationship from the related entity by specifying the primary entity type. So, the 1:N and N:1 relationships are created from a different starting point, but are otherwise the same. We can also create custom N:1 relationships by creating a lookup field on a related entity.

For example, in Microsoft Dynamics CRM 2011, an account can have many contacts associated with it. Each contact can have a parent account. From the point of view of the account, this is a 1:N relationship with contacts, and from the point of view of the contact, this is a N:1 relationship with accounts.

Creating a custom 1:N relationship

To create a custom 1:N relationship, follow these steps:

1. In the navigation pane, click on **Settings**.

2. In the **Customization** group, click on **Customizations** and then click on **Customize the System** to open the default solution.

3. In the left-hand navigation area of the solution, expand the **Entities** component and then expand the appropriate entity.

4. Click on the **1:N Relationships** area.

5. In the grid toolbar, click on **New 1:N Relationship**.

6. In the **New Relationship** pop-up window, provide the following information:

   ° **Primary Entity**: The primary entity from which you want to create a 1:N relationship, for example, Account

   ° **Related Entity**: The entity to which you want to create a 1:N relationship, for example, Policy

 If you are creating a 1:N relationship, the **Primary Entity** field is already selected and is read-only. You can specify the related entity. If you are creating a N:1 relationship, the **Related Entity** field is already selected and is read-only. You can select the primary entity.

- ○ **Name** (in **Relationship Definition**): Schema name of the relationship, for example, `packt_account_packt_policy` is the default name for a custom 1:N relationship between the `account` and `packt_account` entities

- ○ **Display Name**: The name of the lookup field

- ○ **Name** (in **Lookup Field**): Name of the lookup field displayed on the primary record, for example, Policy Holder.

- ○ **Requirement Level**: The requirement level for the lookup field (following options are available for this field):

    No Constraint: It is optional for related records to have a primary record

    Business Required: It is mandatory for related records to have a primary record

    Business Recommended: It is suggested that related records should have a primary record

- ○ **Description**: A description for the lookup field

- ○ **Display Option**: Specifies whether the related records are displayed from the primary record (the following options are available for this field):

    Use Plural Name: The related records are displayed in an area on the primary record using plural name of the related entity as the area label

    Use Custom Label: The related records are displayed in an area on the primary record using a custom label for the area

    Do Not Display: The related records are not displayed on the primary record

    Custom Label: The custom label that is used when **Display Option** is set to **Use Custom Label**

- ○ **Display Area**: The area group on the primary record where the related records are displayed

- ○ **Display Order**: The sort order of the related records area on the primary record

- ○ **Type of Behavior**: The relationship behavior between the two
  entities when certain actions are applied to a primary record
  (see the **Relationship behaviors** section discussed later in this
  chapter) for further details

7. Click on **Save and Close**.

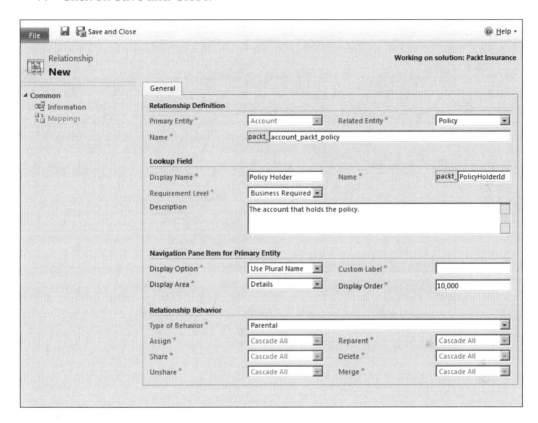

Primary fields as lookup values

A lookup field enables your users to specify the primary record of a related record.
Microsoft Dynamics CRM displays the primary field value of the primary record
in the lookup field, but stores the **global unique identifier** (**GUID**) of the primary
record in the database.

For example, the primary field of the **User** entity is the **Full Name** field. When a user is the owner of a record, the system displays the name of the user in the **Owner** lookup field on the related record, but stores the GUID of the user record in the **Owner** field in the CRM database.

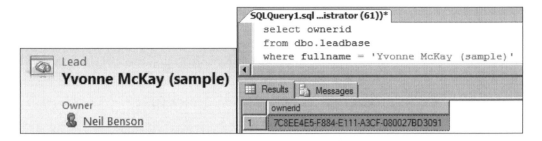

Relationship behaviors

When you carry out certain actions on a primary record, the related records may also be affected depending on the defined relationship behavior between the two entities. The important actions are as follows:

- **Assign**: Changing the owner to another user or team
- **Share**: Sharing the record with another user or team
- **Unshare**: Revoking the sharing with another user or team
- **Reparent**: Associating the record with a new parent record, for example, changing the customer of a case
- **Delete**: Deleting the record
- **Merge**: merging two records (for contacts and accounts)

All other actions—such as activating and deactivating the primary record—have no effect on any related records.

There are four relationship behavior types as follows:

- **Parental**: Any action taken on the primary record is also taken on all related records. For example, if you delete the primary record, all the related records are also deleted. In a parental relationship, the primary and related records are often called the parent and child records.
- **Referential**: Any action taken on the primary record does not affect any related records. If you delete the primary record, the link to that record is removed from the related records.

- **Referential, Restrict Delete**: Any action taken on the primary record does not affect any related records and you cannot delete the primary record while it has one or more related records.

- **Configurable Cascading**: You can define whether actions taken on the primary record are cascaded to the related records or not. The available options are as follows:

  - **Cascade All**: Any action taken on the primary record is also taken on all related records.

  - **Cascade Active**: Any action taken on the primary record is also taken on all active related records — inactive related records are not affected.

  - **Cascade User-Owned**: Any action taken on the primary record is also taken on all related records owned by the same user that owns the primary record.

  - **Cascade None**: Any action taken on the primary record does not affect any related records.

  - **Remove Link**: This option also only applies to the **Delete** action and removes the link between the primary record and all related records.

  - **Restrict**: This option applies only to the **Delete** action and prevents a primary record being deleted when it has one or more related records.

Example of relationship behaviors in an action

The **Opportunity** entity has the entity relationships and relationship behaviors as described in the following table:

Related entity	Relationship behavior	Description
Parent Account (N:1)	Parental	If the parent account is assigned, shared, unshared, reparented, deleted, or merged, the same action will be applied to all opportunities related to the account.
Campaign (N:1)	Referential	If the campaign is assigned, shared, unshared, reparented, deleted or merged, no related opportunities will be affected.

Related entity	Relationship behavior	Description
Order (1:N)	Referential, Restrict Delete	If the opportunity is assigned, shared, unshared, reparented, or merged, no related orders will be affected. However, the opportunity cannot be deleted when it is related to an order.

There are some rules and restrictions on entity relationships in Microsoft Dynamics CRM 2011:

- An entity can have multiple relationships with another entity. Each relationship schema name must be unique.

- To avoid system entities being parented by the custom entities, a custom entity should not be the primary entity in a relationship with a related system entity where the relationship behavior is **Parental**, or where the relationship behavior is **Configurable Cascading** and one of the options is set to **Cascade All**, **Cascade Active**, or **Cascade User-Owned**.

- To avoid the multi-parental relationships, an entity can only be the related entity in one relationship where the relationship behavior is **Parental**, or where the relationship behavior is **Configurable Cascading** and one of the options is set to **Cascade All**, **Cascade Active**, or **Cascade User-Owned**.

- No system entities have a **Configurable Cascading** entity relationship behavior.

- Where two system entities have a **Parental** relationship behavior, you can modify the behavior to **Configurable Cascading**, but not to **Referential, Restrict Delete**.

- The **System** relationship behavior is a special behavior type reserved for some system entity relationships and it cannot be modified or used in the custom relationships.

- Changes to the user interface elements of relationships—such as the display name of the lookup field—must be published before they are applied to the system but schema changes—such as the relationship behavior—do not need to be published.

N:N relationships

In an N:N relationship (also called a many-to-many relationship), a record of one entity can be associated with zero or more records of a second entity, and records of the second entity can be associated with zero or more records of the first entity.

Native and manual N:N relationship types

When an N:N relationship exists between two entities, an intersection entity stores the identifiers of each related record.

The following diagram shows a policy, policy claim, and claim entities. The policy and claim entities have an N:N relationship. A policy can have many claims and a claim can be against many policies. The policy claim entity is the intersection entity that is used to store the identifier of each related policy and claim.

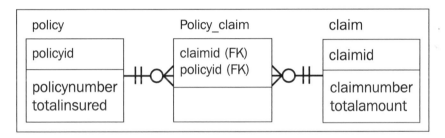

There are many scenarios where native N:N relationships will meet our requirements.

However, in our example, let's say we need to store the value of each policy claim because the total amount of the claim might be split against several different policies. The native N:N policy claim intersection entity is hidden and cannot be customized, so we cannot create a custom attribute on the policy claim entity.

Manual N:N relationships rely on you to create a custom intersection entity with two 1:N relationships that together act as an N:N relationship. Just like any other custom entity, we can see a manual intersection entity in the CRM user interface, we can customize it, and we can interact with it programmatically.

So in our example, instead of creating a native N:N relationship between the policy and claim entities we could create a policy claim entity with the 1:N relationships to the policy and claim entities. Now, we can customize the policy claim entity by creating a policy claim amount field, and any other fields such as the date that the claim became associated with the policy, the status of the policy claim, and so on.

Creating a native N:N relationship

To create a native N:N relationship, follow these steps:

1. In the navigation pane, click on **Settings**.

2. In the **Customization** group, click on **Customizations** and then click on **Customize the System** to open the default solution.

3. In the left-hand navigation area of the solution, expand the **Entities** component and then expand the appropriate entity.

4. Click on the **N:N Relationships** area.

5. In the grid toolbar, click on **New N:N Relationship**.

6. In the **New Relationship** pop-up window, under the **Other Entity** section, provide the entity name of the other entity, with which you want to create the N:N relationship, in the **Entity Name** field.

7. For each entity, provide the following information in the **Current Entity** field:

    ° **Display Option**: This field specifies whether the other entity records are displayed from the current entity record or not. The following options are availabel for this field:

      Use Plural Name: The other entity records are displayed in an area on the current entity record by using plural name of the other entity as the area label.

      Use Custom Label: The other entity records are displayed in an area on the current entity record by using a custom label for the area.

      Do Not Display: The other entity records are not displayed on the current entity record.

      Custom Label: This is the custom label used when the **Display Option** field is set to **Use Custom Label**.

      Display Area: This is the area group on the primary record where the related records are displayed.

    ° **Display Order**: This is the sort order of the related records area on the primary record.

8. In the **Relationship Definition** section, provide the following information:

    ° **Name**: Schema name of the relationship

    ° **Relationship Entity Name**: The name of the hidden intersect entity

9. Click on **Save and Close**.

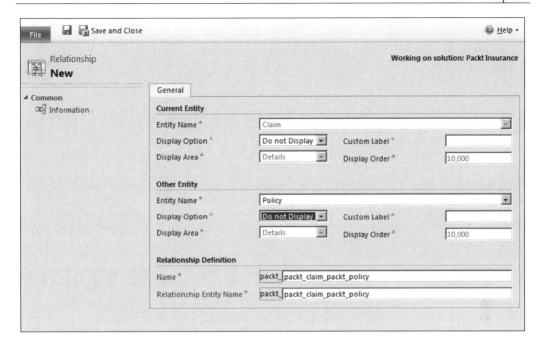

Self-referential relationships

A self-referential relationship is a relationship between an entity and itself. There are two types of self-referential relationships:

- Self-referential 1:N relationships
- Self-referential N:N relationships

Self-referential 1:N relationships

Self-referential 1:N relationships are useful for representing the hierarchical associations between the records, for example, a master order with related sub-orders.

Self-referential 1:N relationships can have a parental relationship behavior. If the relationship behavior is parental, any assign, share/unshare, reparent, delete, or merge action applied to the parent record will also be applied to all its child records.

A self-referential relationship cannot be used to create either direct or indirect circular relationships where the primary record is related to itself or any record in its own hierarchy.

To create a self-referential 1:N relationship, follow the procedure to create a 1:N relationship and specify the primary entity to be the same entity as the related entity.

Self-referential N:N relationships

Self-referential N:N relationships are useful for representing the loose associations between records, for example, cases linked to other cases where the root cause of all cases is the same.

To create a self-referential N:N relationship, follow the same procedure that we discussed earlier in this chapter for creating an N:N relationship and specify the initial entity to be the same entity as the other entity.

Mappings

Entity relationship field mappings reduce the data entry required when new records are created from within the context of a primary record.

For example, when you create a new contact from the **Associated Contacts** view on an **Account** form, some of the data from the account—such as the address and phone number—is copied to similar fields on the new contact record. Mappings in the account-to-contact entity relationship make this possible.

Field values from the primary record are only copied to the related record when the related record is initially created. If the fields in the primary record are later modified, the changes are not copied to the related records.

Creating and modifying mappings

To create or modify the entity relationship field mappings, perform the following steps:

1. In the navigation pane, click on **Settings**.
2. In the **Customization** group, click on **Customizations** and then click on **Customize the System** to open the default solution.
3. In the left-hand navigation area of the solution, expand the **Entities** component and then expand the appropriate entity.
4. Click on the **1:N Relationships** area.
5. Above the actions toolbar, in the **Type** field, select **Mappable**.
6. Double-click on the mappable relationship in which you want to create or modify the mapping.

7. In the **Relationship** form, select **Mappings**.

8. To modify an existing field mapping, delete the existing field mapping and then create a new field mapping.

9. To create a new field mapping, click on **New** in the action toolbar.

10. The **Create Field Mapping** pop-up window shows all the source entity fields and all the unmapped target entity fields. Select the source entity field and target entity field that you want to map, and click on **OK**.

11. Click on **Save and Close** to close the **Relationship** form.

12. Entity relationship field mappings need to be published to take effect. In the **Solution** form, click on **Publish All Customizations** to publish your customizations.

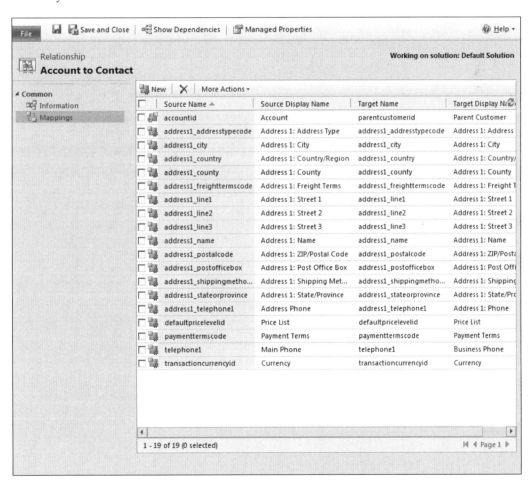

Requirements for mapping

Some requirements must be met before two fields can be mapped:

- Both fields must have the same datatype and format.

- If the fields are text fields, the target field length must be equal to or longer than the source field length.

- If the fields are option sets, the integer value for the source option should match the integer value for the target option, otherwise the option set values will appear to map incorrectly.

- A target field can only be mapped to one source field. If you want to modify the mapping, delete the existing mapping and create a new mapping.

- A source field can be mapped to several target fields.

- Only the editable fields that are published on the form of the source entity can be mapped.

Connections

Connections is a new feature of Microsoft Dynamics CRM 2011 that enables your users to connect two records together by using a connection role that you have defined.

A **connection role** defines the type of relationship between two records and each connection role can have matching connection roles that describe the reciprocal relationship. When we create a connection between two records by using a connection role that has a matching connection role, a reciprocal connection is automatically created.

For example, *Contact A* could be connected to *Contact B* with the *Parent* connection role. The *Child* connection role is a matching connection role of the *Parent* connection role so *Contact B* is automatically connected to *Contact A* with the *Child* connection role.

The connections feature supersedes the relationships feature in previous versions of Microsoft Dynamics CRM.

Creating connection roles

To create a connection role, follow these steps:

1. In the navigation pane, click on **Settings**.

2. In the **Business** group, click on **Business Management** and then click on **Connection Roles**.

3. Click on **New**.

4. Provide the following information:

    ° **Name**: Enter name of the connection role in this field.

    ° **Connection Role Category**: Select the category of the connection role. You can modify the categories by customizing the **Category** global option set.

    ° **Description**: Provide a description for the connection role.

    ° **Select record types**:

        All: The new connection role will be available for connecting all types of records.

        Only these record types: This option enables you to specify which types of records are available when using the new connection role.

5. Click on **Save**.

6. Optionally, click on **Add Existing** in the matching connection roles sub-grid to associate an existing connection role with the new connection role.

7. Click on **Save and Close**.

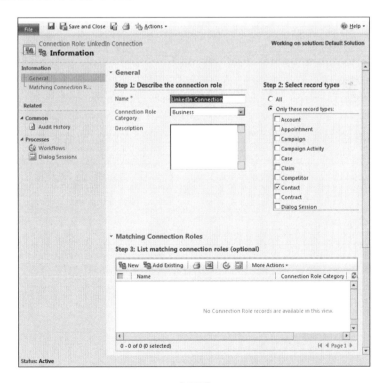

Creating a connection

To create a connection between two records, follow these steps:

1. Navigate to one of the records that you want to create a connection between.

2. In the form ribbon's **Collaborate** group, click on **Connect**.

3. In the **Connection** pop-up window, provide the following information:

    ○ **Name**: Enter name of the record to connect to. You can specify any record for which connections have been enabled.

    ○ **At this role**: The connection role that the records should be connected with.

    ○ **Description**: A description of the connection.

4. Optionally, expand the **Details** tab and provide the following information:

    ○ **At this role**: The reciprocal connection role that the records should be connected with.

    ○ **Start Date**: Start date of the connection.

    ○ **End Date**: End date of the connection.

5. Click on **Save and Close**.

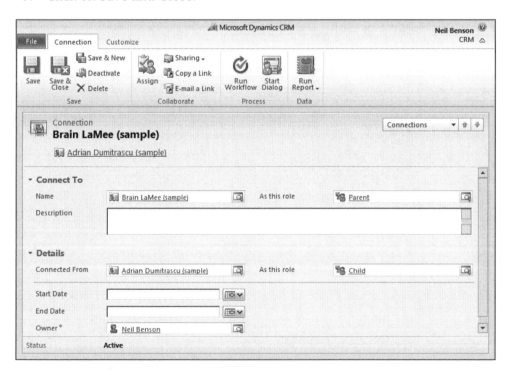

Summary

Here's a quick summary of what we've learned in this chapter.

There are two types of supported entity relationships—1:N (which is the same as N:1) and N:N. The polymorphic and 1:1 entity relationships exist in CRM 2011, but we can't use these relationship types in our customization.

When we create a 1:N custom relationship, the primary field of the related entity is displayed in the lookup field on the primary entity. For example, the **Owner** field on the **Lead** form displays the full name of the owing user because **Full Name** is the primary field of the **User** entity.

We can specify relationship behaviors for our custom 1:N relationships. Behavior types determine what happens to related records when parent records are assigned, shared/ unshared, reparented, deleted, or merge. The available behavior types are as follows:

- **Parental**
- **Referential**
- **Referential, Restrict Delete**
- **Configurable Cascading**

There are two types of N:N relationship. Native N:N relationships are created when we use the standard customization features to create a custom N:N relationship and have hidden intersection entities that cannot be customized. Manual N:N relationships can be created by creating a custom intersection entity with two 1:N relationships.

Native N:N relationships are useful when we need to associate two entities loosely, but do not need to store information about the relationship. Manual N:N relationships are useful where we need to create attributes about the relationship.

A self-referential relationship is a relationship between an entity and itself. Self-referential 1:N relationships are useful for hierarchical associations. Self-referential N:N relationships are useful for loosely associating records of the same type.

Mappings between fields in an entity relationship reduces the need for data entry by copying values from the primary record to the related record. Values are only copied when the related record is created from within the context of the primary record, and are not maintained during subsequent changes to the values in the primary record.

Users can connect two records together by using a connection role that describes the nature of the connection. Connection roles are maintained by the system administrator and can have a matching connection role that describes the reciprocal connection.

Test your knowledge

Q. 1   Which of the following entity relationship types are supported in Microsoft Dynamics CRM 2011 (select all that apply)?

1. N:1 relationships
2. 1:N self-referential relationships
3. 1:N circular relationships
4. 1:1 relationships
5. Manual N:N relationships

Q. 2   A user has reported an error message when trying to delete an account record: "The record could not be deleted because of an association. The record cannot be deleted, because it is associated with another record." What is the likely cause of this message?

1. The account record has a circular relationship with itself.
2. The account entity has a parental relationship with a child entity.
3. The account entity has a referential, restrict delete relationship with a primary entity.
4. The account entity has a referential, restrict delete relationship with a related entity.
5. The account entity has a remove link cascading behavior with a primary entity.

Q. 3   Imagine we have a requirement to store the start date and end date of relationships between contacts, which can each be related to many other contacts. Which of the following features could we use (select two correct options)?

1. Self-referential 1:N contact-to-contact relationship
2. Native N:N contact-to-contact relationship by adding a start date and an end date field to the intersection entity
3. Manual N:N contact-to-contact relationship by adding a start date and an end date field to the intersection entity
4. Circular self-referential 1:N contact-to-contact relationship
5. Connection with a connection role restricted to contact records only

Q. 4   Which of the following statements regarding mappings is/are true (choose all that apply)?

1.   Both mapped fields must be published on the forms of the respective entities.

2.   If the fields are option sets, the option set labels must be matched exactly.

3.   A source field can be mapped to more than one target field, if the source field has the same datatype and format as all the target fields.

4.   Changes to the entity relationship field mappings must be published before they take effect.

5.   Updates to the mapped field values on the primary record will cascade down to a related record until the link is removed between the primary and related record.

Q. 5   Which of the following statements regarding connections is/are true (Choose all that apply)?

1.   Each connection must have a connection role.

2.   Connection roles can be exported as a component in a managed solution.

3.   Only users with sufficient security privileges can use connections.

4.   A connection role can have more than one matching connection role.

5.   Connections can have a start date and an end date.

6

User Interface Customization: Forms, Views, and Charts

So far we've learned about customizing Microsoft Dynamics CRM 2011 using the "behind-the-scenes" techniques such as creating custom entities, attributes, and relationships. In this chapter, we'll focus on customization techniques that make a much bigger impact on your users' experience by learning how to customize forms, views, and charts.

In this chapter we will learn about:

- Customizing forms
- Customizing views
- Customizing charts

So let's get on with it...

Customising forms

A **form** is a web page that is used to display information about a single record. Forms are also used for creating and updating individual records.

There are two form types:

- **Main form**: It is used by the Microsoft Dynamics CRM 2011 web client and Microsoft Dynamics CRM 2011 for Outlook.

- **Mobile form**: It is used by the Microsoft Dynamics CRM 2011 Mobile Express client to display forms on HTML 4.0-compatible mobile devices. Refer to the *Customizing mobile forms* section discussed later in this chapter for more information about Mobile Express and mobile forms.

Components of a form

This section describes the following:

- Components of a main form and main form editor
- Components of a mobile form and mobile form editor

Components of a main form

The following diagram shows the components and layout of a main form:

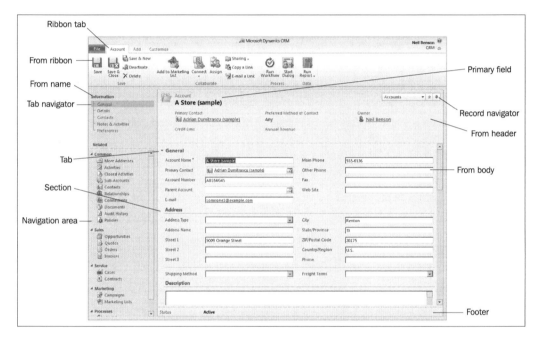

Components of a main form editor

The following diagram shows the components of a main form editor:

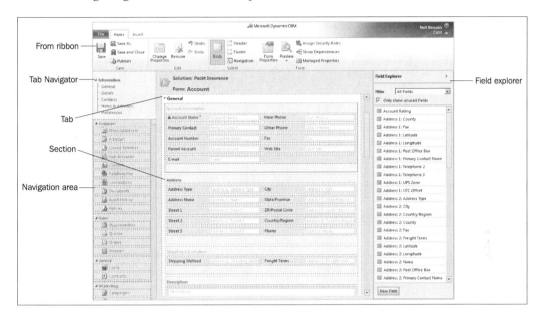

Components of a mobile form

The following diagram shows the components and layout of a mobile form:

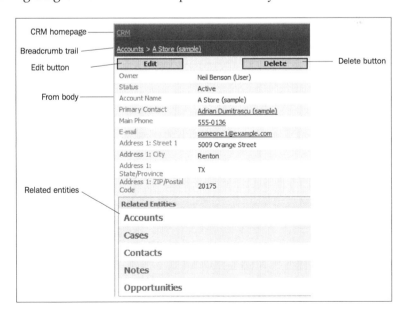

Components of a mobile form editor

The following diagram shows a mobile form editor:

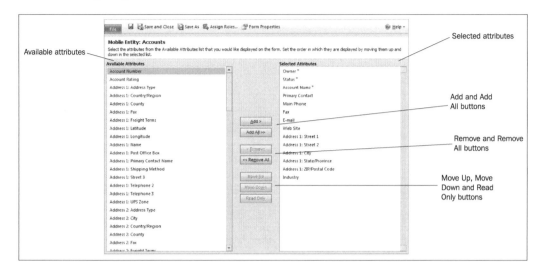

Customizing main forms

Most system entities and all custom entities have at least one form, which can be customized according to your users' requirements.

Some system entities—such as the activity entity—do not have a form at all. Other system entities—such as the case resolution and opportunity close entities—have forms which are not customizable. But the forms for most system entities can be customized.

All custom entities have a customizable form.

In this section, we'll learn about customizing forms by:

- Editing tabs
- Editing sections
- Editing fields
- Editing the navigation area
- Editing the header and footer
- Adding sub-grids
- Adding iFrames

- Adding web resources
- Removing form components
- Previewing forms

>
>
> **Read-optimized forms**
>
> Microsoft Dynamics CRM 2011 Update Rollup 7 was published in March 2012 and introduced a new feature called read-optimized forms. Read-optimized forms display a read-only version of your form without loading the form ribbon or web resources, making it useful for users who open forms to view rather than update records.
>
> Update Rollup 7 was released after MB2-866 was published, so read-optimized forms are unlikely to be included in your exam, and are not covered in this exam certification guide.
>
> You can find out more about read-optimized forms on the CRM team blog at `http://msdn.microsoft.com/en-us/library/hh913610.aspx`.

Editing tabs

A **tab** is a collapsible collection of sections. The tab's label appears in the tab navigator.

Tabs have the following properties:

- **Name**: This field specifies the schema name of the tab used when referring to this tab programmatically.

- **Label**: This field specifies the name of the tab that appears on the form. You can choose whether to show or hide the label on the form.

- **Expanded**: You can choose whether the tab is expanded or collapsed when the form is opened. Frequently used sections are often contained in an expanded tab and infrequently used sections are often contained in a collapsed tab.

- **Visibility**: You can choose whether or not the tab is visible when the form is opened. You could customize the tab using a script to become visible only when certain conditions are met.

- **Columns**: Tabs can have one or two columns, and each column can contain a section. Note that each section contains two columns of fields, so a one-column tab contains two columns of fields and a two-column tab contains four columns of fields. If your tab has two columns, you can choose the percentage width available to each column.

- **Events**: You can associate script libraries with your tab and manage functions that will be called on the `TabStateChange` event.

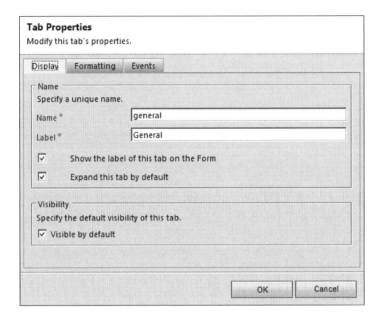

Inserting or modifying a tab

Follow these steps to insert or modify a tab:

1. In the navigation pane, click on **Settings**.

2. In the **Customization** group, click on **Customizations** and then click on **Customize the System** to open the default solution.

3. Expand the **Entities** component and then expand the entity that you want to customize.

4. Click on the **Forms** sub-component and open the form that you want to customize.

5. To insert a new tab, in the form ribbon, click on the **Insert** tab and in the **Tabs** group, click on the **One Column** button to insert a one-column tab or the **Two Column** button to insert a two-column tab.

6. To modify an existing tab, click on the tab that you want to modify and in the form ribbon, click on the **Change Properties** button.

7. In the **Tab Properties** pop-up window, modify the tab's properties according to your requirements.

8. Click on **OK** to close the **Tab Properties** window.

9. Optionally, you can click-and-drag the tab to position it on the form relative to other tabs.

10. In the form ribbon, click on **Save** to save your changes.

11. Click on **Publish** to publish your changes.

Editing sections

A **section** is a collection of fields within a tab.

Sections have the following properties:

- **Name**: This field specifies the schema name of the section used when referring to this tab programmatically.

- **Label**: This field specifies the name of the section that appears on the form. You can choose whether to show or hide the label on the form, and whether to show a line under the label or not.

- **Width**: You can specify the width of the field label area within the section in pixels.

- **Visibility**: You can choose whether or not the section will be visible when the form is opened. You could customize the section that uses a script to become visible only when certain conditions are met.

- **Layout**: You can specify whether your section has one, two, three, or four columns of fields.

- **Field Label Alignment**: You can specify whether the field labels in your section are left-, center-, or right-aligned.

- **Field Label Position**: You can specify whether the field labels in your section are on the left-hand side or above the field.

Note that sections cannot be associated with form scripts.

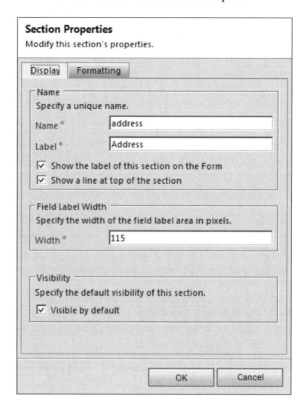

Inserting or modifying a section

Follow these steps to insert or modify a section:

1. In the navigation pane, click on **Settings**.

2. In the **Customization** group, click on **Customizations** and click on
    Customize the System to open the default solution.

3. Expand the **Entities** component and expand the entity that you want
    to customize.

4. Click on the **Forms** sub-component and open the form that you want
    to customize.

5. To insert a new section, follow these steps:

    a. In the form ribbon, click on the **Insert** tab.

    b. In the **Sections** group, click on the **One Column**, **Two Column**,
        Three Column, or **Four Column** button to insert a section with
        the required number of columns.

6. To modify an existing section, follow these steps:

    a. Click on the section that you want to modify.

    b. In the form ribbon, click on the **Change Properties** button.

    c. In the **Section Properties** pop-up window, modify the section's properties according to your requirements.

    d. Click on **OK** to close the **Section Properties** window.

7. Optionally, you can click-and-drag the section to position it on the form relative to other tabs.

8. In the form ribbon, click on **Save** to save your changes.

9. Click on **Publish** to publish your changes.

Editing fields

Fields have the following properties:

- **Label**: this field specifies the field label as it appears on the form. You can choose whether to show or hide the label on the form. By default, the field label on the form is the field's display name. After you change the label, any changes made to the field's display name will not update the field's form label.

- **Field Behavior**: You can specify whether the field is read-only or not. This only applies to the field on this form. The field may be editable on other forms, or it can be updated by synchronizing with CRM for Outlook or updated when records are imported.

- **Locking**: You can specify whether the field can be removed from the form or not.

- **Visibility**: You can specify whether or not the field will be visible when the form is opened.

- **Layout**: You can specify how many columns the field occupies in the section.

- **Events**: You can associate script libraries with your field and manage functions that will be called on the OnChange event.

Lookup fields have the following additional properties:

- **Related Records Filtering**: Provides options that enable you to filter the lookup records displayed to the user.
- **Additional Properties**: Provides options for you to specify whether a search box is displayed or not, the default view for the displayed records is displayed or not, and whether a view selector is displayed or not.

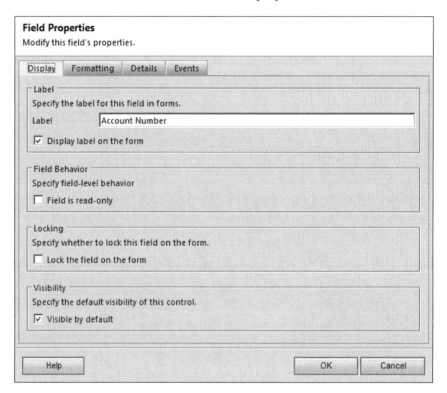

Inserting or modifying a field

Follow these steps to insert or modify a field:

1. In the navigation pane, click on **Settings**.
2. In the **Customization** group, click on **Customizations** and then click on **Customize the System** to open the default solution.
3. Expand the **Entities** component and then expand the entity that you want to customize.

4. Click on the **Forms** sub-component and open the form that you want to customize.

5. To insert a field, follow these steps:

    a. Click on the section into which you want to insert the field.

    b. In **Field Explorer**, double-click on the field that you want to insert.

6. To modify an existing field, follow these steps:

    a. Click on the field that you want to modify.

    b. In the form ribbon, click on the **Change Properties** button.

    c. In the **Field Properties** pop-up window, modify the field's properties according to your requirements.

    d. Click on **OK** to close the **Field Properties** window.

7. Optionally, you can click-and-drag the field to position it in the section relative to other fields.

8. In the form ribbon, click on **Save** to save your changes.

9. Click on **Publish** to publish your changes.

> From **Form Navigator**, you can also create a new field by clicking on the **New Field** button.
>
> The same field can be added to a form more than once.

Editing the navigation area

The **navigation area** displays the relationships for the current entity.

Relationships have the **Label** property. This field specifies the relationship label as it appears on the form. By default, the relationship label on the form is the relationship's display name. After you change the relationship label, any changes made to the relationship's display name will not update the relationship's label on the form.

Inserting or modifying a relationship

Follow these steps to insert or modify a relationship:

1. In the navigation pane, click on **Settings**.

2. In the **Customization** group, click on **Customizations** and then click on **Customize the System** to open the default solution.

3. Expand the **Entities** component and then expand the entity that you want to customize.

4. Click on the **Forms** sub-component and open the form that you want to customize.

5. In the **Select** group in the form editor ribbon, click on **Navigation**.

6. To insert a new navigation, in **Relationship Explorer**, double-click on the relationship that you want to add to the **Navigation** area.

7. To modify an existing relationship, follow these steps:

    a. In the left-hand navigation, select the relationship that you want to modify.

    b. In the form ribbon, click on the **Change Properties** button.

    c. In the **Relationship Properties** pop-up window, modify the relationship's properties according to your requirements.

    d. Click on **OK** to close the **Relationship Properties** window.

8. To remove an existing relationship, follow these steps:

    a. In the left-hand navigation, select the relationship that you want to remove.

    b. In the **Edit** group of the form ribbon, click on **Remove**.

9. Optionally, you can click-and-drag the relationship to position it relative to other relationships.

10. In the form ribbon, click on **Save** to save your changes.

11. Click on **Publish** to publish your changes.

By default, all relationships are already displayed in the navigation area. The only relationships available to insert into the navigation area are the relationships that you have previously removed from the navigation area.

From **Form Navigator**, you can also create a new relationship by clicking on the **New 1:N** or **New N:N** button.

Editing the header and footer

The **form header** and **form footer** are special sections that display important fields while the user scrolls through the body of the form. The fields in the header and footer are read-only.

The header and footer sections have the following properties:

- **Width**: You can specify the width of the field label area within the header and footer in pixels.

- **Layout**: You can specify whether the header or footer has one, two, three, or four columns of fields.

- **Field Label Alignment**: You can specify whether the field labels in your header or footer are left-, center-, or right-aligned.

- **Field Label Position**: You can specify whether the field labels in your header or footer are on the left-hand side or above the field.

Modifying the header or footer

Follow these steps to modify the header or footer:

1. In the navigation pane, click on **Settings**.

2. In the **Customization** group, click on **Customizations** and then click on **Customize the System** to open the default solution.

3. Expand the **Entities** component and then expand the entity that you want to customize.

4. Click on the **Forms** sub-component and open the form that you want to customize.

5. In the form ribbon, click on the **Header** button to modify the header or the **Footer** button to modify the footer.

6. To change the header or footer properties, in the form ribbon, click on the **Change Properties** button.

7. Once you have modified the properties to meet your requirements, click on **OK**.

8. Optionally, you can add, remove, and position fields in the header or footer by using the same procedures as adding, removing, and positioning fields in other sections.

9. In the form ribbon, click on **Save** to save your changes.

10. Click on **Publish** to publish your changes.

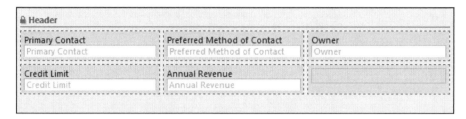

Adding sub-grids

A **sub-grid** displays a list of related records in the main form body. Up to four sub-grids can be displayed on a form.

The properties of a sub-grid are as follows:

- **Name**: This field specifies the schema name of the sub-grid used when referring to this sub-grid programmatically.

- **Label**: This field specifies the label of the sub-grid as it will be displayed on the form. You can choose whether the label is displayed on the form or not.

- **Data Source**: This field specifies the primary data source for the sub-grid.

- **Records**: You can choose whether to display all entities or only entities with a relationship to the current entity.

- **Entity**: This is the entity that will be displayed in the sub-grid.

- **Default View**: This is the default view of the entity that will be displayed in the sub-grid.

- **Additional Options**: You can choose whether or not to display a record search box, the alphabetic index record selector, and the view selector.

- **Chart Options**: You can choose whether to display a chart selector (and a default chart) or show only a specified chart in place of the sub-grid.

- **Layout**: You can specify how many columns the sub-grid occupies in the section.

- **Row Layout**: You can specify how many rows the sub-grid occupies in the section or whether to expand to use available space or not. Only one component on a form can be expanded to use the available space.

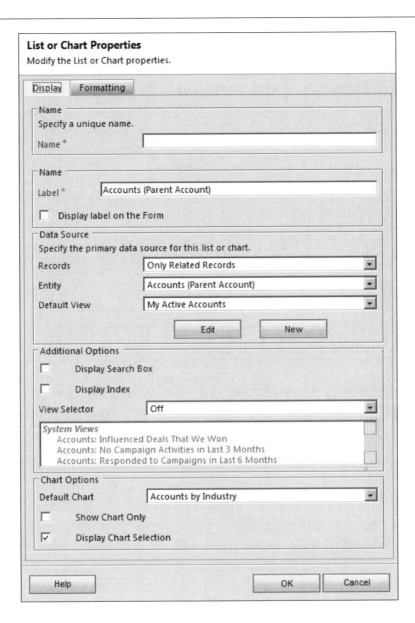

List or Chart Properties
Modify the List or Chart properties.

| Display | Formatting |

Name
Specify a unique name.

Name * [   ]

Name

Label * [Accounts (Parent Account)   ]

☐ Display label on the Form

Data Source
Specify the primary data source for this list or chart.

Records   [Only Related Records   ▾]

Entity   [Accounts (Parent Account)   ▾]

Default View [My Active Accounts   ▾]

[Edit]   [New]

Additional Options

☐ Display Search Box

☐ Display Index

View Selector [Off   ▾]

System Views
  Accounts: Influenced Deals That We Won
  Accounts: No Campaign Activities in Last 3 Months
  Accounts: Responded to Campaigns in Last 6 Months

Chart Options

Default Chart [Accounts by Industry   ▾]

☐ Show Chart Only

☑ Display Chart Selection

[Help]   [OK]   [Cancel]

Inserting or modifying a sub-grid

Follow these steps to insert a sub-grid:

1. In the navigation pane, click on **Settings**.

2. In the **Customization** group, click on **Customizations**, and then click on **Customize the System** to open the default solution.

3. Expand the **Entities** component and then expand the entity that you want to customize.

4. Click on the **Forms** sub-component and open the form that you want to customize.

5. To insert a new sub-grid, follow these steps:

   a. In the form ribbon, click on the **Insert** tab.

   b. Click on the **Sub-Grid** button.

6. To modify an existing sub-grid, follow these steps:

   a. In the form body, click on the sub-grid that you want to modify.

   b. In the form ribbon, click on the **Change Properties** button.

7. In the **List or Chart Properties** pop-up window, modify the sub-grid's properties according to your requirements.

8. Click **OK** to close the **List or Chart Properties** window.

9. Optionally, you can click-and-drag the sub-grid to position it relative to other fields.

10. In the form ribbon, click on **Save** to save your changes.

11. Click on **Publish** to publish your changes.

Adding iFrames

An **iFrame** (also known as an **Inline Frame**) is an HTML document embedded inside a CRM form that is often used to embed content from another source—for example, a map of an account's location—on a form.

iFrames have the following properties:

- **Name**: This is the schema name of the iFrame used when referring to this iFrame programmatically.

- **URL**: This is the locator for the HTML document to be displayed in the iFrame. You can also specify whether or not to pass the record object-type code and unique identifier as parameters.

- **Label**: This is the label of the iFrame with an option of whether to display the label or not.
- **Security**: This field specifies whether to restrict cross-frame scripting or not.
- **Visibility**: This field specifies whether or not the iFrame is visible when the form is opened.

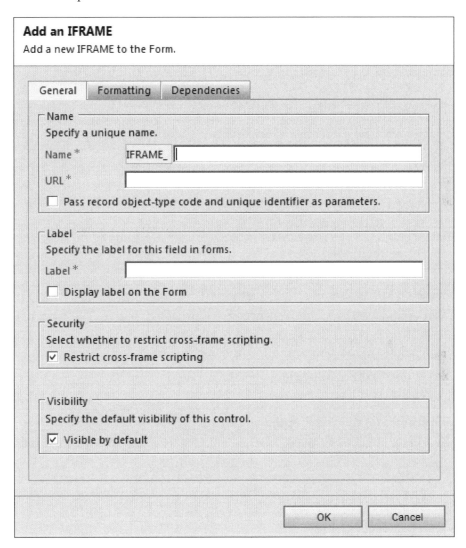

Inserting or modifying an iFrame

Follow these steps to insert or modify an iFrame:

1. In the navigation pane, click on **Settings**.

2. In the **Customization** group, click on **Customizations** and then click on **Customize the System** to open the default solution.

3. Expand the **Entities** component and then expand the entity that you want to customize.

4. Click on the **Forms** sub-component and open the form that you want to customize.

5. To insert a new iFrame, follow these steps:

    a. In the form ribbon, click on the **Insert** tab.

    b. Click on the **iFrame** button.

6. To modify an existing iFrame, follow these steps:

    a. In the form body, click on the iFrame that you want to modify.

    b. In the form ribbon, click on the **Change Properties** button.

7. In the **iFrame Properties** pop-up window, modify the iFrame's properties according to your requirements.

8. Click on **OK** to close the **iFrame Properties** window.

9. Optionally, you can click-and-drag the iFrame to position it relative to other fields.

10. In the form ribbon, click on **Save** to save your changes.

11. Click **Publish** to publish your changes.

Adding web resources

A web resource is a file that can be used to extend or customize Microsoft Dynamics CRM 2011. You can associate the following types of web resources with a form:

* HTML file
* Image file
* JavaScript library
* Silverlight library

Web resources have the following properties:

- **Web resource**: Lookup to an existing form-enabled web resource.
- **Name**: Schema name of the web resource used when referring to this resource programmatically.
- **Label**: This field specifies the label for the web resource on the form. You can choose whether to display the label or not.
- **Visibility**: You can specify whether or not the web resource will be visible when the form is opened.
- **Layout**: You can specify how many columns the web resource occupies in the section.
- **Row Layout**: You can specify how many rows the web resource occupies in the section or whether to expand to use available space or not. Only one component on a form can be expanded to use the available space.
- **Scrolling**: This field specifies whether the web resource always scrolls, never scrolls, or scrolls as necessary.
- **Border**: You can specify whether the web resource has a border or not.

Inserting or modifying a web resource

Follow these steps to add a web resource:

1. In the navigation pane, click on **Settings**.
2. In the **Customization** group, click on **Customizations** and then click on **Customize the System** to open the default solution.
3. Expand the **Entities** component and expand the entity that you want to customize.
4. Click on the **Forms** sub-component and open the form that you want to customize.
5. To insert a new web resource, follow these steps:
   a. In the form ribbon, click on the **Insert** tab.
   b. Click on the **Web Resource** button.
6. To modify an existing web resource, follow these steps:
   a. Click on the web resource that you want to modify.
   b. In the form ribbon, click on the **Change Properties** button.

7. In the **Web Resource Properties** pop-up window, specify the web resource's properties according to your requirements.

8. Click on **OK** to save your web resource properties.

9. Optionally, you can click-and-drag the web resource to position it relative to other fields.

10. In the form ribbon, click on **Save** to save your changes.

11. Click on **Publish** to publish your changes.

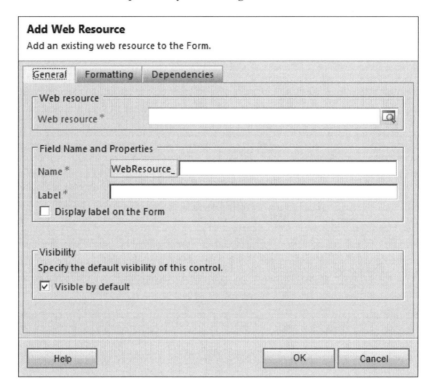

Removing the form components

You can remove tabs, sections, fields, relationships, sub-grids, iFrames, and web resources from a form.

Follow these steps to remove a form component:

1. In the navigation pane, click on **Settings**.

2. In the **Customization** group, click on **Customizations** and then click on **Customize the System** to open the default solution.

3. Expand the **Entities** component and then expand the entity that you want to customize.

4. Click on the **Forms** sub-component and open the form that you want to customize.

5. Select the form component that you want to remove.

6. In the form ribbon, click on the **Remove** button.

7. In the form ribbon, click on **Save** to save your changes.

8. Click on **Publish** to publish your changes.

Warning—removing components

Removing a tab removes all the sections contained within the tab.

Removing a section removes all the fields contained within the section.

Some relationships—such as the activities and closed activities relationships—cannot be easily added back to the navigation area.

Previewing forms

You can preview changes made to your main form before saving and publishing your customizations.

The **Create Form** preview displays the version of the form presented when a new record is created. The **Update Form** preview displays the version of the form presented when an existing record is opened. The primary difference between these preview forms is the execution of script when different versions of the form are opened.

Follow these steps to preview changes made to your form:

1. In the form ribbon of the main form designer, click on **Preview**.

   a. Click on **Create Form** to preview the version of the form presented when a new record is created.

   b. Click on **Update Form** to preview the version of the form presented when an existing record is opened.

   c. Click on **Read-Only Form** to preview the read-only version of the form.

2. Optionally, click on **Simulate Form Save** to execute any scripts attached to the **OnSave** form event.

3. Close the preview form to return to the form designer.

Customizing mobile forms

Microsoft Dynamics CRM 2011 Mobile Express delivers a lightweight CRM web client designed for users using mobile devices that need to read and update CRM records.

In this section we'll learn about:

- Accessing CRM Mobile Express
- Enabling entities for CRM Mobile Express
- Customizing the mobile form fields

Accessing CRM Mobile Express

CRM Mobile Express is delivered to any unsupported browser that accesses the CRM website. At the release of Microsoft Dynamics CRM 2011, only Internet Explorer 7 or above was supported.

For an on-premise deployment, you can also experience the CRM Mobile Express user interface using Internet Explorer by visiting `https://[yourCRMserver]/[yourCRMorgnization]/m/`.

If you are using CRM Online, you can also experience the CRM Mobile Express user interface using Internet Explorer by visiting `http://[yourCRMorganizationURL]/m/`.

Enabling entities for CRM Mobile Express

Only those entities, which have been enabled for Mobile Express, appear in the Mobile Express homepage and related entity views.

Follow these steps to enable an entity for CRM Mobile Express:

1. In the navigation pane, click on **Settings**.
2. In the **Customization** group, click on **Customizations** and then click on **Customize the System** to open the default solution.
3. Expand the **Entities** component and click on the entity that you want to enable for Mobile Express.
4. Under the **General** tab of the entity properties, navigate to the **Outlook & Mobile** section and check the **Mobile Express** checkbox.
5. Click on **Save**.

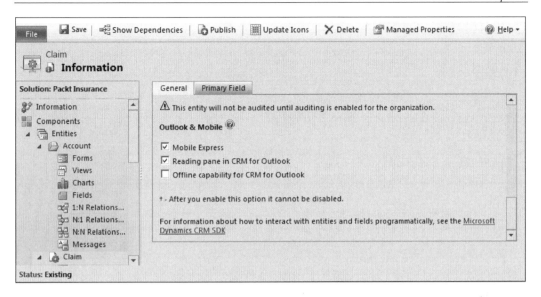

Customizing the mobile form fields

Mobile forms can be edited by using the mobile form designer. For custom entities, the **Name**, **Owner**, and **Status** fields are added to the **Information** mobile form by default.

Follow these steps to customize a mobile form:

1. In the navigation pane, click on **Settings**.

2. In the **Customization** group, click on **Customizations** and click on **Customize the System** to open the default solution.

3. Expand the **Entities** component and then expand the entity that you want to customize.

4. Click on the **Forms** sub-component and open the mobile form that you want to customize.

5. In the **Available Attributes** pane, select fields that you want to be displayed on the mobile form and click on **Add**.

6. In the **Selected Attributes** pane, select fields that you do not want to be displayed on the mobile form and click on **Remove**.

7. In the **Selected Attributes** pane, you can use the **Move Up** and **Move Down** buttons to position fields according to your requirements and use the **Read Only** button to disable fields in the form **Edit** mode.

8. In the form ribbon, click on **Save** to save your changes.

9. Click on **Publish** to publish your changes.

Creating forms

In the previous section we learned how to customize the existing forms. In this section we'll learn about:

- Creating a main form
- Creating a mobile form

Creating a main form

Almost all system and all custom entities have a main form called **Information**. You can create additional forms to meet the needs of different groups of users.

Follow these steps to create a new main form:

1. In the navigation pane, click on **Settings**.

2. In the **Customization** group, click on **Customizations** and then click on **Customize the System** to open the default solution.

3. Expand the **Entities** component and expand the entity that you want to customize.

4. Click on the **Forms** sub-component, click on **New**, and select **Main Form**.

5. Customize the form according to your requirements.

6. In the form ribbon, click on **Save As** and provide a name and description for your custom form.

7. Click on **OK** and then close the form designer.

8. Click on your entity and then click on the **Publish** button to publish your changes.

 When you create a new main form, the form is role-based and only users with the System Customizer or System Administrator roles are able to display the form. You must assign the form to other roles, for other users to be able to display your new form.

Selecting a form

If you have created an additional form for an entity, the users are presented with a form selector when they open a record of the entity. The form selector appears just above the tab navigator in the top-left corner of the form.

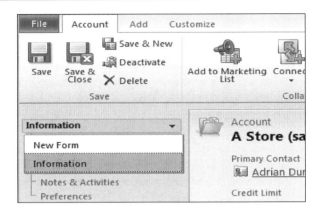

The CRM system remembers which form the user has selected, and will present the same form each time the user opens a record until the user change his/her preference in the form selector.

You can restrict which forms should be available to a user using the role-based forms feature. See the *Role-based forms* section discussed later in this chapter.

Creating a mobile form

Microsoft Dynamics CRM 2011 Mobile Express also supports multiple mobile forms.

Follow these steps to create a mobile form:

1. In the navigation pane, click on **Settings**.
2. In the **Customization** group, click on **Customizations** and then click on **Customize the System** to open the default solution.
3. Expand the **Entities** component and then expand the entity that you want to customize.
4. Click on the **Forms** sub-component, click on **New**, and select **Mobile Form**.
5. Customize the form according to your requirements.
6. In the form toolbar, click on **Information**.
7. Provide a name and description for your custom form.
8. Click on **Save** and then close the form designer.
9. Click on your entity and then click on the **Publish** button to publish your changes.

Role-based forms

The role-based forms feature enables you to create multiple main and mobile forms for an entity and restricts each form to users with specified security roles.

For example, you might have a version of *an account* form that displays information pertinent to a customer service representative, which is different to the information needed by a sales representative.

> Users can see all the fields for an entity by using features such as Advanced Find. The role-based forms feature is a convenient method for hiding fields from forms, but not a secure method for restricting sensitive fields. If you need to restrict sensitive fields from being viewed by some users, use the Field-Level Security feature.

Fallback form

When you use the role-based forms feature, there must always be one form that is enabled for **fallback**, that is, a form that is displayed to users who do not have a security role that enables them to view any of the other role-based forms.

You can restrict which security roles have access to a form even when your entity has only one form, but the same form will also be used as the fallback form and displayed to all users who do not have one of the specified security roles.

Therefore, from a practical viewpoint, you need at least two main forms to use the role-based forms feature.

Creating a role-based form

Follow these steps to create a role-based form:

1. In the navigation pane, click on **Settings**.
2. In the **Customization** group, click on **Customizations** and then click on **Customize the System** to open the default solution.
3. Expand the **Entities** component and then expand the entity that you want to customize.
4. Select the **Forms** sub-component.
5. In the forms grid, select a main form and click on the **Assign Security Roles** button in the actions toolbar.

6. In the **Assign Security Roles** pop-up window, choose either **Display to everyone** or **Display only to these selected security roles**. Then, select the security roles that you want to be able to view this form.

7. Optionally, check **Enabled for fallback**, if you want this form to be the default form displayed to users who do not have one of the specified security roles.

8. Click on **OK**.

9. Click on your entity and then click on the **Publish** button to publish your changes.

Users that possess one of the selected security roles will be able to use your role-based forms in addition to the fallback form.

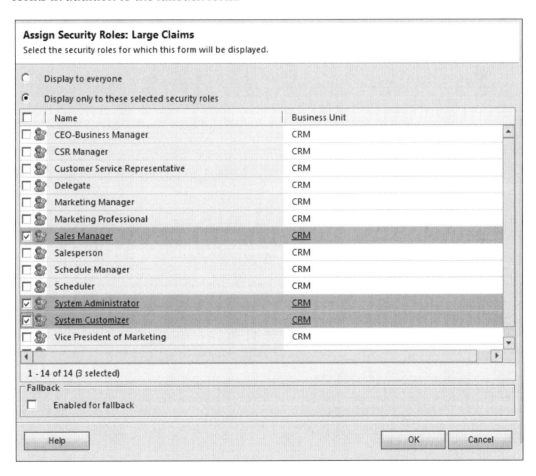

Ordering forms

When there are multiple forms available for a user to choose from, you can specify the order of the forms in the form selector.

Follow these steps to modify the form order:

1. In the navigation pane, click on **Settings**.

2. In the **Customization** group, click on **Customizations** and then click on **Customize the System** to open the default solution.

3. Expand the **Entities** component and expand the entity that you want to customize.

4. Select the **Forms** sub-component.

5. In the forms grid, select a main form and click on the **Form Order** button in the actions toolbar.

6. In the **Form Order** pop-up window, select a form and use the up and down arrow keys to specify the form order to meet your requirements.

7. Click on **OK**.

8. Click on your entity and then click on the **Publish** button to publish your changes.

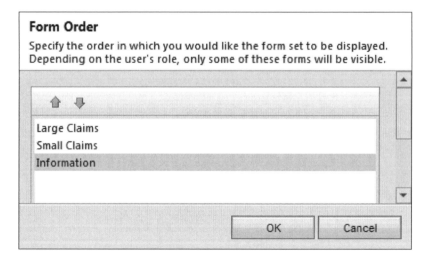

Customizing views

A **view** displays a filtered list of records displayed in rows with columns displaying field values.

There are two types of views:

- **System views**: These are defined for each entity within a solution and are usually customizable by system administrators and system customizers, but cannot be deleted.

- **User views**: These are created by users by using Advanced Find and can be assigned to or shared with other users or teams.

All custom entities and almost all system entities have several system views that can be customized to meet your requirements. You can modify most system views and create new custom system views. When customizing a view, you can change the filter criteria and the columns displayed.

In this section we'll learn about:

- Creating a system view
- Organizing data in a view
- Adding and maintaining fields in a view
- Selecting a default view

System views

Each entity has several system views. System views can be modified (with some restrictions), but they cannot be deleted.

Active and inactive record views

The active view and inactive view display all active or all inactive records. You can modify the view names and descriptions of the active and inactive record views as well as the columns displayed, column widths, sort order, and filter criteria.

The active and inactive views are both public views and are displayed in the list of system views in the view selector in the entity grid from the main application navigation area. All custom views that you create in a solution are also public views.

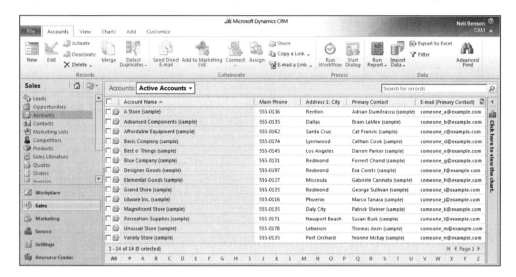

Advanced Find view

The Advanced Find view displays the results of an Advanced Find query. You can modify the view name and description of the Advanced Find view as well as the columns displayed, column widths, sort order, and filter criteria.

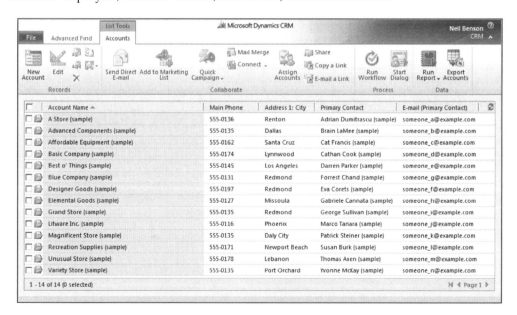

Associated view

The associated view is selected from the form navigation area of a primary record and displays all the related records of the current record. For example, when you select the **Contacts** area in the form navigation of the **Account** form, the **Contacts Associated View** defines how the account's related contacts are displayed in the grid.

You can modify the view name and description of the associated view as well as the columns displayed, column widths, sort order, and filter criteria. By default, only active-related records are displayed.

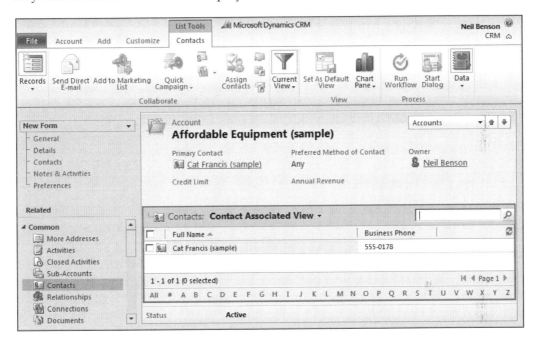

Lookup view

The lookup view displays the results of a lookup query in a **Look Up Record** window. You can modify the view name and description of the lookup view as well as the columns displayed, column widths, sort order, and filter criteria. The entity's primary field (usually the **Name** field) must be displayed as the first column in the view. By default, only active related records are displayed.

Searchable fields in Lookup and Quick Find views

The searchable fields for the lookup view are the same as those defined for the Quick Find view.

Quick Find view

The Quick Find view defines the searchable fields and the records displayed when a user searches for records by using the Quick Find feature.

You can modify the view name and description of the Quick Find view as well as the columns displayed, column widths, sort order, and filter criteria. By default, only active related records are displayed.

Searchable fields in Lookup and Quick Find views

The searchable fields for the Quick Find view also define the searchable fields for the lookup view.

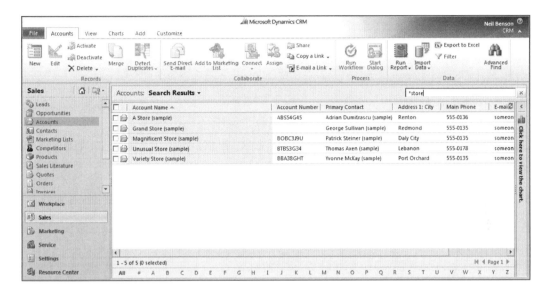

Creating a view

You can create custom views to meet your users' requirements.

Follow these steps to create a new view:

1. In the navigation pane, click on **Settings**.

2. In the **Customization** group, click on **Customizations** and then click on **Customize the System** to open the default solution.

3. Expand the **Entities** component and expand the entity that you want to customize.

4. Select the **Views** sub-component.

5. In the action toolbar, click on **New**.

6. In the **View Properties** pop-up window, provide a name and a description for your view.

7. Click on **OK**.

8. In the **View Customization** pop-up window, follow the procedures discussed in the next section to edit the view's filter criteria and columns.

9. Click on **Save and Close**.

10. Click on your entity and then click on the **Publish** button to publish your changes.

Organizing data in a view

You can apply filter criteria to custom views or modify the filter criteria of system views to organize the data displayed in a view.

Follow these steps to modify a view's filter criteria:

1. In the navigation pane, click on **Settings**.

2. In the **Customization** group, click on **Customizations** and then click on **Customize the System** to open the default solution.

3. Expand the **Entities** component and expand the entity that you want to customize.

4. Select the **Views** sub-component and open the view that you want to customize.

5. Click on the **Edit Filter Criteria** button.

6. In the **Edit Filter Criteria** pop-up window, modify the filter criteria to meet your requirements.

7. Click on **OK**.

8. Optionally, modify the view name to describe the filter applied to the records.

9. Click on **Save and Close**.

10. Click on your entity and then click on the **Publish** button to publish your changes.

Adding and maintaining fields in a view

You can add and remove the columns displayed in a view, modify the column widths, and specify the sort order.

Follow these steps to modify a view's fields:

1. In the navigation pane, click on **Settings**.

2. In the **Customization** group, click on **Customizations** and then click on **Customize the System** to open the default solution.

3. Expand the **Entities** component and expand the entity that you want to customize.

4. Select the **Views** sub-component and open the view that you want to customize.

5. To add columns:

   Click on the **Add Columns** button, select the fields that you want to add and then click on **OK**. Optionally, you can change the **Record Type** and select columns from any primary entity for your current entity.

6. To move a column:

   Select the column and then click on the left or right arrow.

7. To modify a column's width:

   Select the column and click on the **Change Properties** button, then specify the required width and click on **OK**.

8. To modify the view's sort order:

   Click on the **Configure Sorting** button and specify the **Sort By** and **Then By** fields and whether the sort order for each is ascending or descending, and then click on **OK**.

9. Click on **Save and Close**.

10. Click on your entity and then click on the **Publish** button to publish your changes.

Selecting a default view

Every entity must have a default view. This is the view that is displayed when a user navigates to the entity's grid from the main application navigation area.

Follow these steps to modify the default view:

1. In the navigation pane, click on **Settings**.

2. In the **Customization** group, click on **Customizations** and then click on **Customize the System** to open the default solution.

3. Expand the **Entities** component and then expand the entity that you want to customize.

4. Select the **Views** sub-component.

5. Select a public view and in the **More Actions** menu on the actions toolbar, select **Set Default**.

6. Click on your entity and then click on the **Publish** button to publish your changes.

Customizing charts

A **chart** is a graphical visualization of data in your CRM system. Using charts can help your users understand large volumes of data to gain insight and enable them to make smarter business decisions rapidly.

Charts are based on a single record type and are generated from the current list of records. So, changing the view associated with the chart will update the chart, and drilling into the chart will update the list of associated records.

In this section we'll learn about:

- Chart types
- Creating a system chart
- Importing and exporting charts

Chart types

There are two types of charts in Microsoft Dynamics CRM 2011:

- **System charts**: These are created by a system administrator or system customizer as a solution component and are available to all users in the organization.

- **User charts**: These are created by a user and are available to that user or any other user or team that the chart is assigned to or shared with.

Creating a system chart

System charts are organization owned and cannot be assigned to or shared with a user or team. Although all users in the organization can display the chart, the content of the chart depends on the users' security privileges.

Chart improvements

The area chart type and multi-series charts were the chart feature improvements introduced with Microsoft Dynamics CRM Update Rollup 5, published in December 2011. The MB2-866 exam was written before Update Rollup 5 was published, so the exam questions are unlikely to examine the area chart type or multi-series charts.

Adding charts to entities

Follow these steps to add a chart to an entity:

1. In the navigation pane, click on **Settings**.

2. In the **Customization** group, click on **Customizations** and click on **Customize the System** to open the default solution.

3. Expand the **Entities** component and then expand the entity that you want to customize.

4. Select the **Charts** sub-component.

5. In the actions toolbar, click on **New**.

6. In the **Chart Designer** pop-up window, select a view used for chart preview.

7. Select a field to display in the **Legend Entries (Series)** — for column charts this is the vertical or Y-axis of your chart. If your series is a numeric field, you can set the aggregate value to **Count: All**, **Count: Non-empty**, **Avg**, **Max**, **Min**, or **Sum**. If your series is a non-numeric field, you can set the aggregate value to **Count: All** or **Count: Non-empty**.

8. Optionally, click on the **Add** a series button to add another series. Your chart can have up to five series and one category or one series and two categories.

9. To change the chart type for a series, click on the **Current chart type** button and select a chart type.

10. To display only the top or bottom records for a series, click on the **Top/Bottom Rules** button and select or clear the rule to meet your requirements.

11. Select a field to display in **Horizontal (Category)**. If your category is a date-time field, you can group the records by **Day**, **Week**, **Month**, **Quarter**, **Year**, **FiscalPeriod**, or **FiscalYear**.

12. Optionally, click on the **Add a category** button to add another category. Your chart can have up to five series and one category or one series and two categories.

13. The chart name is automatically derived from the series and categories that you have selected. Optionally, you can rename the chart.

14. Optionally, add a description to describe the purpose of the chart.

15. Click on **Save and Close**.

16. Click on your entity and click on the **Publish** button to publish your changes.

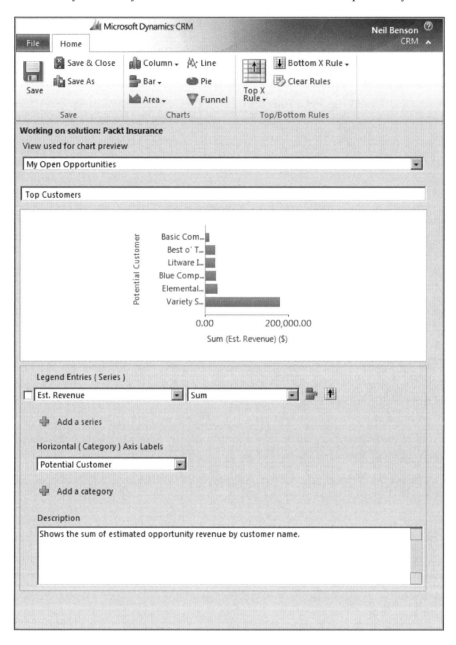

Selecting a chart type

The available chart types are listed in the following table:

Chart type	Description	Example
Column	Displays each category in a vertical column with the height of the column representing the series aggregate	
Bar	Displays each category in a horizontal bar with the length of the bar representing the series aggregate	
Area	Emphasizes changes in values between categories by shading the area beneath the line connecting the series data points	
Line	Emphasizes changes in values between categories by connecting the series data points with a line	

Chart type	Description	Example
Pie	Emphasizes the proportion of each category by displaying the series data points as segments of a pie	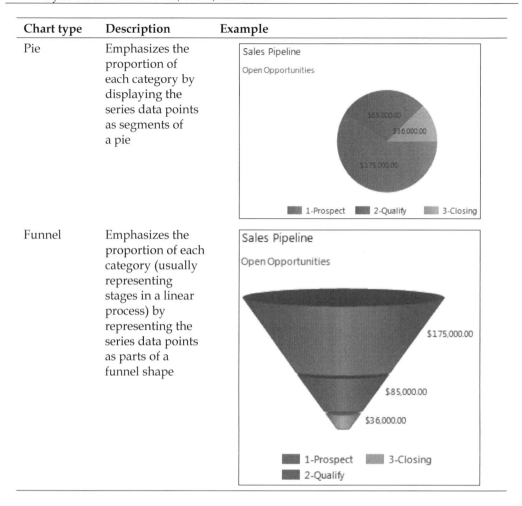
Funnel	Emphasizes the proportion of each category (usually representing stages in a linear process) by representing the series data points as parts of a funnel shape	

Optionally, items in a bar, column, or area chart can also be stacked (or 100% stacked).

Exporting and importing charts

Charts can be exported from and imported into Microsoft Dynamics CRM.

System charts can be exported, modified, and reimported. This is a useful technique for making advanced customizations to the chart XML, which cannot be achieved with the Chart Designer feature.

User charts can be exported and then reimported as a system chart. This is a useful technique for making a user's user chart available to all other users as an organization-owned system chart.

Exporting a system chart

Follow these steps to export a system chart:

1. In the navigation pane, click on **Settings**.

2. In the **Customization** group, click on **Customizations** and then click on **Customize the System** to open the default solution.

3. Expand the **Entities** component and expand the entity that you want to customize.

4. Select the **Charts** sub-component and select the chart that you want to export.

5. In the actions toolbar, click on **More Actions** and then select **Export Chart**.

6. Open or save the exported chart XML file.

> **Customizing the chart XML**
>
> Customizing the chart XML is beyond the scope of MB2-866. Please refer to the Microsoft Dynamics CRM 2011 SDK for further information (http://msdn.microsoft.com/en-us/library/gg327901.aspx).

Exporting a user chart

Follow these steps to export a user chart:

1. In the navigation pane, navigate to the entity grid.

2. Expand the chart viewer and select the user chart that you want to export.

3. In the main application ribbon, select the **Charts** tab and then click on the **Export Chart** button.

4. Open or save the exported chart XML file.

Importing a chart as a system chart

Follow these steps to import a system chart or a user chart as a system chart:

1. In the navigation pane, click on **Settings**.

2. In the Customization group, click on **Customizations** and then click on **Customize the System** to open the default solution.

3. Expand the **Entities** component and expand the entity that you want to customize.

4. Select the **Charts** sub-component.

5. In the actions toolbar, click on **More Actions** and then select **Import Chart**.

6. In the **Import Chart** pop-up window, click on **Browse**, select the chart's XML file from your computer, and click on **Open**.

7. Click on **OK**.

Summary

Here's a quick recap of what we've learned in this chapter:

A form is a web page used to create, update, and view information about a single record. There are two form types—main form (used in the CRM web client and CRM for Outlook) and mobile form (used in the CRM Mobile Express client).

Most system entities and all custom entities have at least one main form that can be customized. You can preview the create, update, and read-only versions of a form. Mobile forms can also be customized.

Role-based forms enable you to create multiple forms for an entity and restrict access to users with specified security roles. There must always be one form enabled for fallback, which is the form displayed to users who do not have a security role that enables them to view any of the role-based forms.

If users have access to multiple forms, you can reorder the forms in the form selector.

A view displays a filtered list of records displayed in rows with columns displaying field values. There are two view types—system views and personal views.

Most system entities and all custom entities have several important system views. There are several customization features available for views.

A chart is a graphical visualization of data in your CRM system. There are two categories of charts—system charts and user charts.

Charts are based on a view. Aggregate options can be applied to chart series depending on whether the series field is numeric or non-numeric. Grouping options can be applied chart categories, if the category field is a date-time field.

System charts can be exported, modified, and reimported. This is a useful technique for making advanced customizations to the chart XML that cannot be achieved with the Chart Designer feature.

User charts can be exported and then reimported as a system chart. This is a useful technique for making a user's user chart available to all other users as an organization-owned system chart.

Test your knowledge

Q. 1   Which of the following properties of a lookup view can be customized (select all those apply)?

1. Column widths

2. First column

3. Row colors

4. Sort order

5. Filter criteria

Q. 2   Which of the following form components can be associated with a form event (select two correct options)?

1. Fields

2. Tabs

3. Header

4. Navigation area

5. Sections

Q. 3   How can user charts be converted into system charts?

1. User charts cannot be converted into system charts.

2. Click on the **Convert to System Chart** button in the **Charts** tab.

3. Click on the **Export Chart** button in the **Charts** tab and then click on the **Import Chart** button in the solution.

4. Click on the **Save As** button in Chart Designer and select the **System Chart** option.

5. User charts are automatically converted to system charts when a user dashboard is converted into a system dashboard.

Q. 4   Which of the following web resources can be added to a form (select all that apply)?

1.   ASPX page

2.   Image file

3.   JavaScript library

4.   Silverlight library

5.   Dynamic link library (DLL)

Q. 5   The form that is displayed to users who do not have a security role that enables them to view a role-based form is called:

1.   Default form

2.   Non-secure form

3.   Restart form

4.   Rollback form

5.   Standard form

Q. 6   For a non-numeric field used as a series in a chart, the aggregate options are (select two):

1.   Count: All

2.   Count: None

3.   Count: Non-empty

4.   Count: Non-null

5.   Count: Null

7
Auditing

Auditing enables you to record and examine changes made to records in Microsoft Dynamics CRM. You may need to audit changes to CRM data to meet legal or regulatory requirements or to meet your organization's security or compliance policies.

In this chapter you will learn how auditing works, how to configure the standard auditing features, how to use the audit logs as records are changed, and how to manage the audit logs as they grow over time. A self-test section at the end of the chapter will test your knowledge.

In this chapter we will cover:

- What is auditing?
- Configuring auditing
- Auditing user access
- Viewing audit data
- Audit permissions
- Managing the audit log

What is auditing?

In Microsoft Dynamics CRM 2011, the auditing feature logs changes that are made to your customer records so that you can review those changes later. The auditing feature is designed to meet the auditing, compliance, security, and governance policies of many regulated enterprises.

The audit logs help you answer questions such as:

- Who updated this field value on this record, and when?
- What was the previous field value before it was updated?
- What actions has this user taken recently?
- Who deleted this record?

What can be audited?

The following operations can be audited:

- Create, update, and delete operations on records.
- Changes to the sharing privileges of a record.
- The N:N association or disassociation of records.
- Changes to security roles.
- Audit changes at the entity, attribute, and organization level. For example, enabling audit on an entity.
- Deletion of audit logs.
- When (date/time) a user accesses Microsoft Dynamics CRM data, for how long, and from what client. See the *Auditing user access* section in this chapter.

Limitations on auditing

The auditing feature does not track the read operations, that is, when a user views a record by any means (forms, views, charts, reports, Advanced Find, or Export to Excel), no audit operation is recorded in the audit log.

The audit data is not available for reporting, querying with Advanced Find, or exporting to Excel.

Auditing is available for all custom and most customizable entities, but auditing is not supported on the note and attachment entities.

Auditing is not available for most customization changes such as creating, modifying, or deleting a solution component.

Audit Summary View and Audit History View are not customizable.

Configuring auditing

In this section, we'll discuss the settings that are needed to configure the auditing feature to meet your requirements.

There are three steps required to configure auditing in Microsoft Dynamics CRM 2011:

1. Configuring organization-level auditing.
2. Configuring entity-level auditing.
3. Configuring field-level auditing.

Configuring organization-level auditing

Auditing is turned off by default and you must start the auditing feature if you need to track changes in the CRM records. You can also stop the auditing feature, if you need to.

To start or stop the organization-level auditing, follow these steps:

1. In the navigation pane, click on **Settings**.
2. In the **System** group, click on **Auditing**.
3. Click on **Global Audit Settings**.
4. Under the **Auditing** tab in the **System Settings** pop-up window, check the **Start Auditing** checkbox to start auditing or uncheck the **Start Auditing** checkbox to stop auditing.
5. Optionally, check or uncheck the **Common Entities** checkbox to start or stop the entity-level auditing for the following entities:
    - Account
    - Contact
    - Goal
    - Goal metric
    - Lead
    - Marketing list
    - Product
    - Quick campaign
    - Rollup query
    - Sales literature

6. Optionally, check or uncheck the **Sales Entities** checkbox to start or stop the entity-level auditing for the following entities:

    ° Competitor

    ° Invoice

    ° Opportunity

    ° Order

    ° Quote

7. Optionally, check or uncheck the **Marketing Entities** checkbox to start or stop the entity-level auditing for the campaign entity.

8. Optionally, check or uncheck the **Customer Service Entities** checkbox to start or stop the entity-level auditing for the following entities:

    ° Case

    ° Contract

    ° Service

9. Click on **OK**.

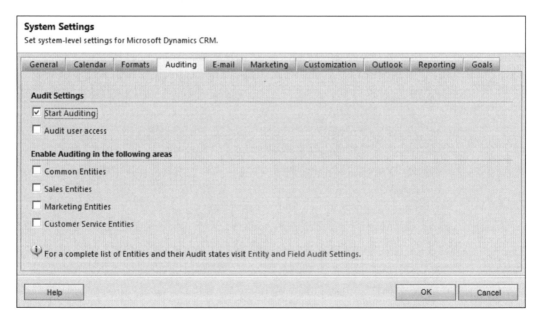

Organization-level auditing tips

Some of the organization-level auditing tips are as follows:

- If you have added a custom entity to the **Sales, Marketing**, or **Customer Service** areas, auditing for that entity will also start or stop if you check or uncheck the **Sales Entities, Marketing Entities**, or **Customer Service Entities** checkboxes.

- If you have added a custom entity to the **Workplace** area, auditing for that entity will not start or stop if you check or uncheck the **Common Entities** checkbox.

- The **Common Entities, Sales Entities, Marketing Entities**, or **Customer Service Entities** checkboxes may already be checked if you have already enabled auditing at the entity level for any of the entities associated with these options.

- If you have checked the **Start Auditing** checkbox, but you have not checked one of the **Common Entities, Sales Entities, Marketing Entities**, or **Customer Service Entities** checkboxes or have started auditing for an entity, the organization-level auditing is enabled but auditing is not started for any entity.

Configuring entity-level auditing

After you have configured organization-level auditing, you can start or stop auditing for individual entities.

To start or stop auditing for an entity, follow these steps:

1. In the navigation pane, click on **Settings**.
2. In the **System** group, click on **Auditing**.
3. Click on **Entity and Field Audit Settings**.
4. In the **Default Solution** pop-up window, expand the **Entities** component. In the **Entities** grid screen, you can review **Audit Status** for all your entities.
5. Select the entity for which you want to start or stop auditing.
6. In the entity's **Data Services** section, check the **Auditing** checkbox to start auditing or uncheck the **Auditing** checkbox to stop auditing.
7. Click on **Save** to save your changes.

When auditing is enabled for an entity, all changes to all the entity's fields are recorded in the audit log. This volume of data can quickly fill the audit log and make it harder to find important entries. You can stop auditing on the entity's other fields, if you require auditing only on specific fields.

Configuring field-level auditing

After you have configured entity-level auditing, you can start or stop auditing for individual fields.

To start or stop auditing for a field, follow these steps:

1. In the navigation pane, click on **Settings**.
2. In the **System** group, click on **Auditing**.
3. Click on **Entity and Field Audit Settings**.
4. In the **Default Solution** pop-up window, expand the **Entities** component.
5. Expand the entity that contains the field for which you want to start or stop auditing.
6. Click on the entity's **Fields** component. In the **Fields** grid screen, you can review **Audit Status** for all your fields.
7. Open the field for which you want to start or stop auditing.
8. In the **Auditing** radio button, select **Enable** to start auditing or **Disable** to stop auditing.
9. If you select the **Disable** option, click on **OK** to acknowledge that by disabling auditing some change in history data may be lost.
10. Click on **Save and Close**.

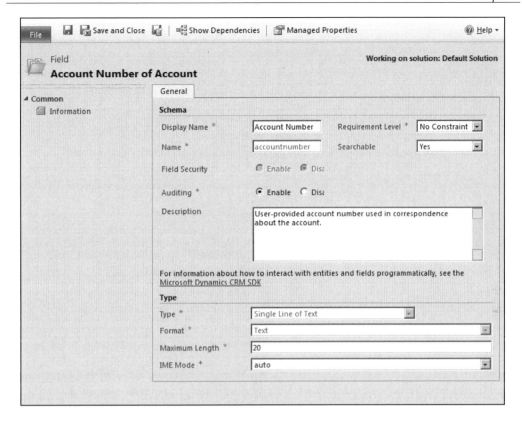

Auditing user access

If the organization-level auditing is enabled, you can record when a user logs in to Microsoft Dynamics CRM in your audit log by enabling user access auditing. The audit log of the user access is available in the **Audit Summary View** page.

Auditing user access

The user access auditing feature was introduced in Update Rollup 7 for Microsoft Dynamics CRM, published in February 2012. The MB2-866 exam was written before Update Rollup 7 was published, so the exam questions are unlikely to examine the user access auditing feature.

To start or stop the user access auditing, follow these steps:

1. In the navigation pane, click on **Settings**.

2. In the **System** group, click on **Auditing**.

3. Click on **Global Audit Settings**.

4. Under the **Auditing** tab in the **System Settings** pop-up window, check the **Audit user access** checkbox to start user access auditing or uncheck the **Audit user access** checkbox to stop user access auditing.

5. Click on **OK**.

Viewing the audit data

In this section, we'll learn the two methods available for viewing the audit data:

- Audit Summary View
- Audit History View for records

Audit Summary View

Audit Summary View provides a filterable list of the system-wide audited operations so that you can quickly find the changes that you need to review.

To display the **Audit Summary View**, follow these steps:

1. In the navigation pane, click on **Settings**.

2. Then in the **System** group, click on **Auditing**.

3. Click on **Audit Summary View**.

4. Optionally, filter on:

   ° The **Changed Date** column to see the operations performed on a particular date or period.

   ° The **Event** column to see all the instances that a particular action was performed.

   ° The **Changed By** column to see all the operations performed by a particular user.

   ° The **Entity** column to see all the operations performed on a particular record type.

- ○ The **Operation** column to see the **Create**, **Update**, or **Delete** operations. Select the **Access** option to see when a user logged in to Microsoft Dynamics CRM.

Audit History View for records

Audit History View for a record provides a filterable list of audited operations to the record so that you can see which field values have been changed over time.

To display the **Audit History View** for a record, follow these steps:

1. Navigate to and open the record you want to review.

2. In the record's navigation area, under the **Common** group, select **Audit History**.

3. Optionally, filter on a particular field to review only the audited operations on that field.

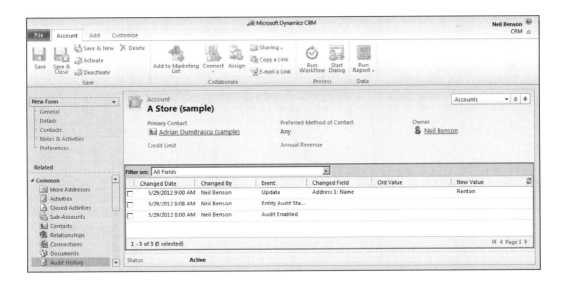

Audit permissions

As a system administrator, you have all the necessary privileges for managing the auditing feature. In this section, we'll discuss the security privileges required for users with other security roles to complete the audit-related tasks.

Audit-related tasks and required privileges

The following table describes the required privileges for the audit-related tasks:

Task	Required privilege
Start or stop the organization-level auditing	Organization: Read and Write
Start or stop the entity-level auditing	Entity: Read and Write
Start or stop the field-level auditing	Field: Read and Write
Start or stop the user access auditing	Organization: Read and Write
View audit summary	Audit Summary View
View audit history for records	Record: Read
	Audit History View
Manage audit logs	View Audit Partitions
	Delete Audit Partitions

Managing the audit log

Audit operations are stored in an audit log. A separate audit log is created every three months. Over time, these audit logs can consume a significant amount of storage on your database server (for the CRM on-premise deployments) or your allocated storage space (for the CRM Online deployments). If database storage is a concern, you can delete the audit logs when it is no longer necessary to store them according to your organization's record retention policy.

Deleting multiple audit logs

You can only delete the oldest audit log. Repeat the following procedure, if you wish to delete more than one audit log.

To delete an audit log, follow these steps:

1. In the navigation pane, click on **Settings**.
2. Then in the **System** group, click on **Auditing**.
3. Click on **Audit Log Management**.
4. Select the oldest audit log and click on the **Delete Logs** button.
5. In the confirmation message, click on **OK**.

Audit logs in the database

Audit operations are stored in the non-customizable audit system entity.

An audit log in Microsoft Dynamics CRM represents a logical collection of audit operations. How audit logs are managed depends on which version of Microsoft SQL Server is deployed.

Microsoft Dynamics CRM 2011 uses Microsoft SQL Server as its database management system. Three editions of Microsoft SQL Server 2008 are supported—Standard, Enterprise, and Datacenter.

For on-premise deployments that use Microsoft SQL Server 2008 Enterprise or Datacenter editions, and for Microsoft Dynamics CRM Online, audit operations are stored in physical database partitions. A new physical partition is created every three months. Each partition acts like a separate table which ensures that the performance of the auditing feature isn't affected too much as the database grows. Each partition represents an audit log in Microsoft Dynamics CRM 2011 and is measured in kilobytes.

Microsoft SQL Server 2008 Standard Edition does not support database partitions so for on-premise deployments that use Microsoft SQL Server 2008 Standard edition audit operations are stored in the CRM organization database. An audit log in Microsoft Dynamics CRM 2011 represents a collection of audit operations grouped by calendar quarter and is measured in rows.

Microsoft SQL Server 2012

Support for Microsoft SQL Server 2012 Standard, Business Intelligence and Edition editions was introduced with Update Rollup 6 for Microsoft Dynamics CRM 2011 in January 2012.

The MB2-866 exam was published before Microsoft SQL Server 2012 or Update Rollup 6 for Microsoft Dynamics CRM 2011 were released, so questions about audit partitions related to Microsoft SQL Server 2012 are unlikely.

Questions about audit partitions related Microsoft SQL Server 2008 are still possible.

Summary

Auditing enables you to record and examine changes made to the records in Microsoft Dynamics CRM.

Auditing does not start by default. Auditing needs to be configured at the organization, entity, and field levels.

Audit Summary View and **Audit History View** are two methods for viewing audit data. The audit data cannot be used in reports, queried in Advanced Find, or exported to Excel.

Audit Summary View provides a filterable list of the system-wide audited operations. The options to filter by are **Changed Date**, **Event**, **Changed By**, **Entity**, and **Operation**.

Audit History of an audited record is a filterable list of the audited operations on the record. There is an option to filter by auditable field.

The audit data is stored in an audit log. A separate audit log is created every three months. Over time, audit logs can consume significant amounts of storage time. The oldest audit log can be deleted when it is no longer required.

The audit logs are stored in a physical database partition when using Microsoft SQL Server 2008 Enterprise or Datacenter editions or Microsoft Dynamics CRM Online. When using Microsoft SQL Server 2008 Standard edition, the audit operations are stored in the CRM organization database and displayed as grouped by calendar quarter.

Various security privileges are available to control which security roles can:

- Start or stop the organization-level, entity-level, and field-level auditing
- View the audit summary and audit history views
- View and delete the audit logs

Test your knowledge

Q. 1   If the **Start Auditing** option is not enabled, which of the following statements is/are true (select all that apply)?

1.   Entity-level and field-level auditing can be configured but will not start.

2.   Entity-level and field-level auditing can be configured and will start.

3.   The Audit Summary View cannot be used.

4.   User access auditing can be configured and will start.

5.   Audit logs cannot be deleted.

Q. 2   Which of the following statements regarding the auditing feature of Microsoft Dynamics CRM is/are true (select all that apply)?

1.   Auditing can be started for several entities at once by multi-selecting entities from the Entities component of a solution and selecting Enable Auditing from the More Actions menu.

2.   The audit history for a record can be filtered by auditable field.

3.   Auditing can be stopped for several fields at once by multi-selecting fields from the Fields component of an entity and selecting Disable Auditing from the More Actions menu.

4.   Auditing can track which records have been opened by a user.

5.   The Audit Summary View is not customizable.

Q. 3   Audit logs can be:

1.   Disabled

2.   Queried

3.   Exported

4.   Deleted

5.   Shrunk

8
Solutions

In this chapter, we will learn about solutions. We will also discuss how we can export and import managed and unmanaged solutions and how solutions are combined when multiple solutions are imported into an organization. You will also discover how to use managed solutions to prevent the solution from being customized further. A self-test section at the end of this chapter will test your knowledge.

In this chapter we will cover:

- Introduction to solutions
- Working with solutions
- Exporting and importing solutions
- Updating managed solutions

Introduction to solutions

A **solution** is a package of customized components that can be imported into a Microsoft Dynamics CRM 2011 system. Each solution has a name, version number, and publisher who owns the solution.

There are two primary purposes to using solutions:

- **Promoting your own customizations**: Solutions can be exported from one Microsoft Dynamic CRM 2011 organization and imported into another. This is useful for promoting your customizations through your development, testing, and production deployments.

- **Obtaining independent software vendor (ISV) solutions**: Solutions containing custom components can also be developed by third-party independent software vendors and imported into your organization. Solutions—whether they are free, for purchase or subscription—can be downloaded from the Microsoft Dynamics Marketplace or directly from ISVs' websites.

Default solution

A **default solution** is installed with every CRM 2011 organization, however, only imported solutions are shown in the solutions area so the default solution is not displayed here.

To view the default solution, perform the following steps:

1. In the navigation pane, click on **Settings**.

2. In the **Customization** group, click on **Customizations** and then click on **Customize the System** to open the default solution.

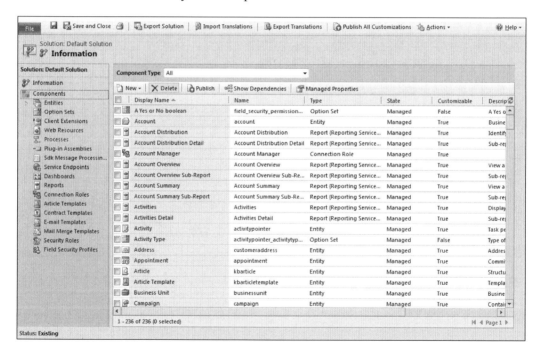

Solution components

A **solution** is a package of components, containing one or more of the following component types:

- Entities
- Option sets
- Client extensions
- Web resources
- Processes
- Plug-in assemblies
- SDK message processing steps
- Service endpoints
- Dashboards
- Reports
- Connection roles
- Article templates
- Contract templates
- E-mail templates
- Mail merge templates
- Security roles
- Field security profiles
- System settings

Customizations not included in solutions

Several configuration settings and customizations are not included in solutions and need to be managed separately. Those are as follows:

- Business units
- Teams
- Users
- Product catalog
- Duplicate detection settings and rules
- Data maps
- Organization-level audit settings
- Document management settings

Unmanaged and managed solutions

Solutions can be packaged as unmanaged or managed solutions. This package type is important as it determines how Microsoft Dynamics CRM handles the solution and, therefore, what you can do with the solution.

Later in this chapter, we will learn how Microsoft Dynamics CRM 2011 handles scenarios when multiple unmanaged or managed solutions are imported into the organization.

Unmanaged solutions

Until you export it, an unmanaged solution does not contain actual solution components; it simply contains references to the actual solution components, which exist in the default solution.

All solutions are initially created as unmanaged solutions.

Unmanaged solutions can be exported from a source organization and imported into a target organization, but unmanaged solutions cannot be deleted.

Managed solutions

Managed solutions isolate the solution components within the managed solution. Publishers can lock down components by configuring the managed properties within a managed solution to prevent the components from being further customized when the managed solution is imported into a new organization.

Managed solutions are created when a solution is exported from a source organization. Unlike unmanaged solutions, managed solutions can be deleted from the target organization.

Working with solutions

In this section, we'll learn more about how we can work with solutions.

In this section we'll cover:

- Creating a solution
- Deleting a solution
- Working with solution components
- Managed properties

Creating a solution

You can create a new solution to contain your customizations.

To create a new solution, follow these steps:

1. In the navigation pane, click on **Settings**.
2. In the **Customization** group, click on **Solutions**.
3. Click on the **New** button.
4. In the **New Solution** pop-up window, provide the following information:

   ○ **Display Name**: This is the friendly name for your solution. The display name will be copied without punctuation or special characters to the **Name** field, which is the schema name for the solution.

   ○ **Publisher**: This field specifies the person, department, or company who published the solution.

   ○ **Version**: This field specifies the version number for your product in the `major.minor.build.revision` format.

   ○ **Configuration Page**: After creating your solution and uploading a HTML web page as a web resource, you can update your solution to refer to this page as a configuration page that will provide additional configuration instructions or options.

   ○ **Description**: This is an optional description of your solution.

5. Click on **Save**.

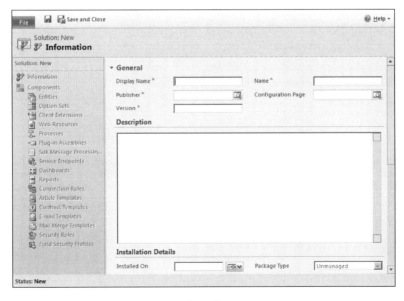

When you create a solution, it is an unmanaged solution. You cannot create a managed solution. You can convert an unmanaged solution to a managed solution when you export it.

Solution publisher

A **publisher** is the person, department, or company that develops and publishes a solution. Solutions from the same publisher are handled in a special way when they are imported into the same organization, so you should use a consistent name for your publisher.

To create a new publisher, follow these steps:

1. In the navigation pane, click on **Settings**.
2. In the **Customization** group, click on **Customizations**.
3. Click on **Publishers**.
4. In the **Publishers** grid, click on **New**.
5. In the **New Publisher** form, provide the following information:
    - **Display Name**: This is the friendly name for the publisher. The display name will be copied without punctuation to the **Name** field, which is the schema name for the publisher.
    - **Description**: This field contains a description of the publisher.
    - **Prefix**: This field contains two to eight alphanumeric characters used as the prefix for entities and fields created by the publisher.
    - **Option Value Prefix**: This field contains a number between 10,000 and 99,999 used as a prefix for option values created by the publisher.
    - **Contact Details**: This field provides the contact details for the publisher.

6. Click on **Save and Close**.

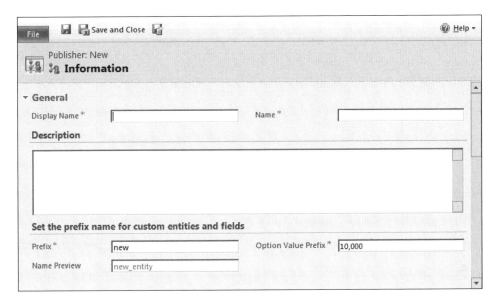

Deleting a solution

There is a significant difference between deleting a managed solution and deleting an unmanaged solution.

An unmanaged solution's components are just references that point to components that actually exist in the default solution. So when you delete an unmanaged solution, the components still exist in the default solution and it is only the unmanaged solution's container and the references that are deleted.

A managed solution's components exist in the solution itself (unless you've added components from another solution), so when you delete a managed solution the solution's container and the actual components are irreversibly deleted.

To delete a solution, follow these steps:

1. In the navigation pane, click on **Settings**.
2. In the **Customization** group, click on **Solutions**.
3. Select the solution and click on the **Delete** button.
4. Click on **OK** to confirm deletion.

Working with solution components

In this section, we'll learn about solution components and discuss how we can work with them.

A **solution component** is a customized element of Microsoft Dynamics CRM.

You can either create new solution components in your unmanaged solution, or you can add existing components from the default solution, or other unmanaged or managed solutions to your unmanaged solution.

Solution components can also be removed or deleted from unmanaged solutions.

Warning – removing and deleting components

When you delete a solution component, it is physically deleted from the database and cannot be easily recovered. Deleting an entity deletes all records of that entity and deleting a field deletes all values of that field, so take special care when deleting entities and fields.

When you remove a component from your solution, the component still exists. It continues to exist either in the default solution or the managed solution from which you referenced it.

Creating new components

You can only create new components to an unmanaged solution.

To add a solution component, follow these steps:

1. In the navigation pane, click on **Settings**.
2. In the **Customization** group, click on **Solutions** and open the appropriate solution.
3. In the **Components** grid toolbar, click on **New** and select the appropriate component type, for example, **Entity**, **Option Set**, or **Web Resource**.
4. Provide the required information for the component type. Refer to the appropriate section, if you need help in understanding how to create a type of component.
5. Click on **Save and Close**.
6. Depending on the type of solution component that you have created, you may need to click on **Publish** to make your changes available.

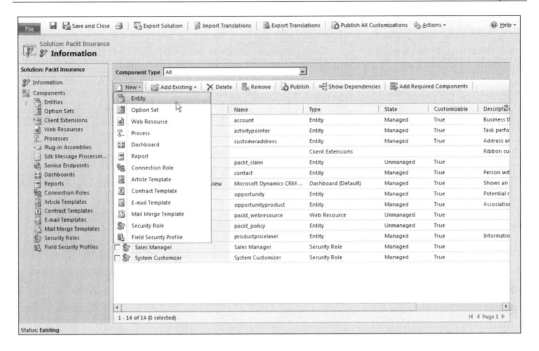

Components in an unmanaged solution actually exist in the default solution.
So creating a new component in your unmanaged solution is the same as creating
the component in the default solution and adding it to your solution.

Deleting components

You can delete custom components that you have created in your solution or
that you have added from another solution.

To delete a component, follow these steps:

1. In the navigation pane, click on **Settings**.

2. In the **Customization** group, click on **Solutions** and open the
   appropriate solution.

3. In the left-hand navigation, click on the appropriate component type
   and select the component that you want to delete.

4. In the components grid toolbar, click on the **Delete** button.

5. In the **Confirm deletion** pop-up window, click on **OK**.

Adding existing components

You can add existing components from the default solution or other managed/ unmanaged solutions to your unmanaged solution. For example, if you want to customize the account entity or the Microsoft Dynamics CRM Overview dashboard, you could add these components to your solution.

To add an existing component, follow these steps:

1. In the navigation pane, click on **Settings**.
2. In the **Customization** group, click on **Solutions** and open the appropriate solution.
3. In the **Components** grid toolbar, click on **Add Existing** and select the appropriate component type, for example, **Entity**, **Option Set**, or **Web Resource**.
4. In the **Select solution components** pop-up window, select the component that you want to add to your solution.
5. Click on **OK**.

Removing components

You can remove any component that has been created in, or added to, your unmanaged solution.

To remove a component, follow these steps:

1. In the navigation pane, click on **Settings**.
2. In the **Customization** group, click on **Solutions** and open the appropriate solution.
3. In the **Components** grid, select the component that you want to remove and in the grid toolbar, click on **Remove**.

Although the components have been removed from your unmanaged solution, they still exist either in the default solution or the solution from which they were added.

Exporting solutions

An exported solution is a ZIP file containing all the solution's components in XML format. Exported solution files can be imported into other CRM organizations. This is the most common method for promoting customizations from development to test to production. It is also the method by which customizations are packaged by publishers and delivered to customers.

When you export a solution from Microsoft Dynamics CRM 2011, you have the option to export the solution as either an unmanaged or managed solution. A managed solution cannot be exported from your organization after it has been imported.

If you export your solution as an unmanaged solution, you will be able to continue customizing the solution's components after importing it into your target organization. If you export your solution as a managed solution, your ability to customize the solution's components will be restricted (depending on the managed properties specified in the solution when it was exported).

Managed solutions in production

Once you have a managed solution in your production environment, there is no easy way to convert it into an unmanaged solution so that you can modify its components. The only supported method involves deleting the managed solution from your production organization, which deletes your production data. It is, therefore, important to understand and consider all the consequences of using managed solutions in your production organization.

How to export a solution

In this section, we'll learn how to export a solution.

When you export your unmanaged solution, only published customizations are included in the solution package. So the first step in the export procedure is to publish your customizations.

To export a solution, follow these steps:

1. In the navigation pane, click on **Settings**.
2. In the **Customization** group, click on **Solutions**.
3. Select the unmanaged solution that you want to export, and in the action toolbar, click on **Export**.
4. In the **Export Solutions** pop-up window, click on the **Publish All Customizations** button and then click on **Next**.
5. If your solution includes system entities or custom entities that have dependencies on other components, the dependent components will be shown in the **Export Solution** pop-up window and included in your exported solution. Click on **Next**.

6. Optionally, select any system settings to be included in your exported solution and then click on **Next**.

7. Select **Package Type** as **Unmanaged** or **Managed**, and click on **Export**.

8. A ZIP file will be available to be opened or saved on your computer.

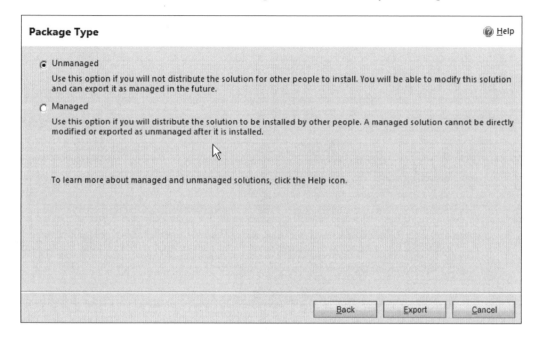

After you export a solution as managed, you cannot install it in the same organization that you exported it from. You can only import a managed solution into a different organization.

Managed properties

The purpose of a managed solution is to allow your solution to be imported into a target organization in a locked state so that no further changes can be made to it. However, there may be scenarios when you want to allow some components of the managed solution to be updated. You can achieve this by modifying the managed properties of the solution's components before exporting the solution.

- Entities and attributes each have several managed properties.

- Most other solution components have a single managed property—they can be customized.

Modifying managed properties

To review or modify the managed properties of a solution component, follow these steps:

1. In the navigation pane, click on **Settings**.

2. In the **Customization** group, click on **Solutions** and open the appropriate solution.

3. Select a solution component and in the **Components** grid toolbar, click on **Managed Properties**.

4. In the **Managed Properties** pop-up window, modify the component's properties to meet your requirements.

5. Click on **OK**.

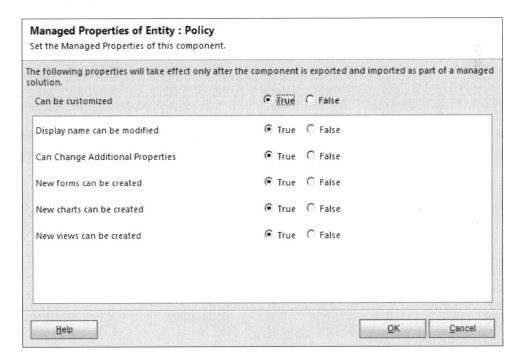

The following table lists the solution components and the managed properties that you can modify:

Solution component	Managed property
Entities	Can be customized
	Display name can be modified
	Can change additional properties
	New forms can be created
	New charts can be created
	New views can be created
Fields	Can be customized
	Display name can be modified
	Can change requirement level
	Can change additional properties
Entity Relationships	
Forms	
Charts	
Views	
Option Sets	
Web Resources	
Processes	
Plug-in Assemblies	Can be customized
SDK Message Processing Steps	
E-mail Templates	
Knowledgebase Article Templates	
Contract Templates	
Mail Merge Templates	
Dashboards	
Security Roles	

Importing solutions

In this section we'll learn about:

- How to import a solution
- Conflict resolution strategies
- The import log file

How to import a solution

To import a solution, follow these steps:

1. In the navigation pane, click on **Settings**.

2. In the **Customization** group, click on **Solutions**.

3. In the **Solution** action toolbar, click on the **Import** button.

4. In the **Import Solution** pop-up window, click on **Browse**, locate the solution file (`.zip` or `.cab` file) on your computer, and click on **Next**.

5. Optionally, click on the **View solution package details** button, and then click on **Next**.

6. Optionally, check the option **Activate any processes and enable any SDK message processing steps included in the solution**. Most solutions will not function correctly until the workflow, dialog, and plug-in components are enabled, but you can choose to enable these components manually later. Click on **Next**.

7. Once the solution import process is complete, optionally click on **Download Log File** to view the result details, and then click on **Close**.

Conflict resolution strategies

The effect of importing a managed solution is different from importing an unmanaged solution and the effects are different on different types of solution components. It is important to understand these differences.

When you import a solution that modifies an existing solution component that has already been customized, there is a potential conflict to resolve.

Microsoft Dynamics CRM 2011 uses two strategies to resolve these conflicts:

- Merge
- Top wins

Merge

The merge strategy applies only to user interface components—ribbons, forms, and views. For user interface components, the merge strategy means that the application's final behavior is calculated from the default solution, then from managed solutions, and finally from unmanaged solutions.

The merge strategy is illustrated in the following diagram:

In the preceding merge conflict resolution example, the *Business Phone* field label on the contact form has been customized in three conflicting solutions—*Solution A (Managed)*, *Solution B (Unmanaged)*, and *Solution C (Managed)*. However, for user interface components, the merge conflict resolution strategy dictates that the unmanaged customization is resolved last and so what users see is determined by the label in *Solution B (Unmanaged)* even though it was installed before *Solution C (Managed)*.

Top wins

The top wins strategy applies to all solution components except user interface components (ribbons, forms, and views). For these components, the application's final behavior is calculated from the default solution, then it is calculated from managed and unmanaged solutions in the order they were imported. Any conflict is resolved in favor of the customization that was applied last.

The top wins strategy is illustrated in the following diagram:

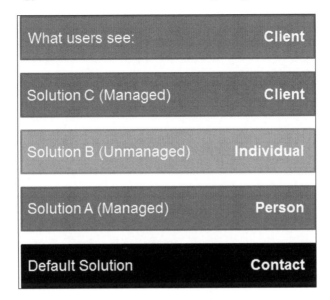

In the preceding top wins conflict resolution example, the display name of the contact entity has been customized in three conflicting solutions—*Solution A (Managed)*, *Solution B (Unmanaged)*, and *Solution C (Managed)*. For entity components the top wins conflict resolution strategy dictates that the conflict is resolved in favor of the solution that was imported last and so what users see is determined by the label in *Solution C (Managed)*.

Remembering the conflict resolution strategies

We can remember the merge strategy with the following mnemonic:

Many Urgent Inquiries Don't Seem to Matter Utterly

Merge (User Interface) – Default Solution, then Managed, then Unmanaged.

We can remember the top wins strategy with the following mnemonic:

Today Will My Urgent Orders Increase?

Top Wins – Managed and Unmanaged – by Order Installed.

Special conflict resolution for updates to managed solutions

The merge conflict resolution strategy dictates that customizations in the unmanaged layer are resolved in favor of customizations in managed solutions. As a consequence, user interface customizations in managed solutions may not be applied because of the unmanaged customizations to the same user interface components.

To relieve this potential problem, when you install an update to a managed solution, you can choose whether to maintain or overwrite any customizations that you have applied in the unmanaged solutions.

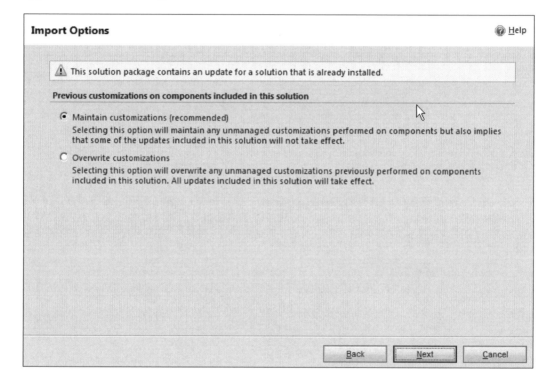

A managed solution is considered to be an update to an existing solution, if it has the same solution name and publisher as an existing managed solution.

Import log file

An option in the last step of the solution import procedure is to download the import log file.

The following screenshot shows the log file for a successful import job:

Solution	
Name	Packt
Display Name	Packt Insurance
Description	
Version	1.0.0.1
Package Type	Unmanaged
Publisher	
Name	packtpublishing
Display Name	Packt Publishing
Description	
E-mail	
Web Site	
City	
Country/Region	
Street 1	
Street 2	
ZIP/Postal Code	
State/Province	
Phone	
Status	Processed
Message	Customizations have been imported successfully.
Progress [%]	100.00
Duration [s]	30.6

The import log file is useful if you need to troubleshoot errors with your solution import job.

For example, imagine the scenario where you have developed a custom *Policy* entity containing a whole number field called *Policy Number*. You have exported your solution as a backup of your customization in progress. Later you discover that the *Policy Number* field needs to be a single line of text, so you delete the *Policy Number* whole number field and create a new text field with the same name.

Now if you import your backup solution, an error message will be displayed.

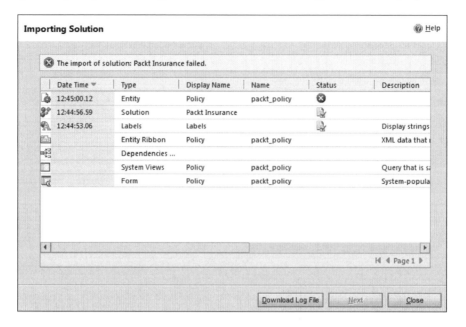

The solution import log will contain information that will explain why the import failed so that you can take steps to resolve the issue.

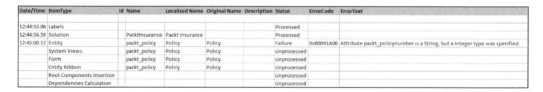

Summary

Here's a quick recap about what we've learned about solutions.

A **solution** is a package of customized components that can be imported into a Microsoft Dynamics CRM 2011 system. Each solution has a name, version number, and publisher who owns the solution. Solutions are used for promoting customizations from one organization to another, or installing customizations provided by a software vendor.

A solution must have a publisher. This is the person, department, or company that develops and publishes the solution. The publisher defines the prefix used for custom entities and fields, and the option value prefix.

A default solution is installed with every CRM 2011 organization. It contains all the system entities.

We can create new solutions. When we create a new solution, it is unmanaged and does not have any solution components. We can either create new solution components or add components from other solutions.

An unmanaged solution's components are just references that point to components which actually exist in the default solution. When you delete an unmanaged solution, the solution container and its references are deleted but the customizations still exist in the default solution.

The result of deleting a managed solution is different. Unless you have added components from another solution, a managed solution's components exist in the solution itself. When you delete a managed solution, the solution container and the actual components are irreversibly deleted.

A solution component is a customized element of Microsoft Dynamics CRM. You can create new solution components and add references to components in other solutions.

Solution components can be deleted or removed. When a component is deleted, it is irreversibly deleted from the solution in which it was created. When a component is removed, the reference to the component is removed from your solution but the component still exists in the solution in which it was created.

Usually, the components of a managed solution cannot be customized. However, you can modify the managed properties of your solution's components before you export the solution as a managed solution to enable components to be further customized according to your requirements.

You can export solutions so that you can promote your published customizations from development to test to production environments or to package customizations for delivery to your customers.

Managed solutions can be customized after being imported into your target organization, but managed solutions cannot (unless you have modified the solution component's managed properties). You cannot install a managed solution into the same organization from which it was exported.

The merge strategy is applied only to user interface components—ribbons, forms, and views. For user interface components, the merge strategy means that application's final behavior is calculated from the default solution, then from the managed solutions, and finally from the unmanaged solutions. We can remember the merge strategy with the following mnemonics:

- Many Urgent Inquiries Don't Seem to Matter Utterly
- Merge (User Interface) – Default Solution, then Managed, then Unmanaged

The top wins strategy applies to all solution components except user interface components. For these components, the application's final behavior is calculated from the default solution, then from the managed and unmanaged solutions in the order they were imported. Any conflict is resolved in favor of the customization that was applied last. We can remember the merge strategy with the mnemonic:

- Today Will My Urgent Orders Increase?
- Top Wins – Managed and Unmanaged – by Order Installed

When you install an update to a managed solution, you can choose whether to maintain or overwrite any customizations that you have applied in the unmanaged solutions.

When you import solution, the final step of the solution import wizard will display the results of the import procedure. To help you troubleshoot any issues, you can download the solution import log file, which will provide a more detailed explanation of the error.

Test your knowledge

Q. 1   To create a managed solution (choose one):

    1.   Choose **Managed** as the solution type when exporting an unmanaged solution.

    2.   Choose **Managed** as the solution type when creating a new solution.

    3.   Use the **Convert to Managed** feature on the **Solution** grid action toolbar.

    4.   Export the solution as an unmanaged solution and edit the `<solutiontype>` property in the solution XML file.

Q. 2   Which of the solution's components can the publisher of a managed solution enable for customization (select all that apply)?

    1.   Reports

    2.   Security roles

    3.   Connection roles

    4.   System settings

    5.   Client extensions

Q. 3   Which of the following are properties of a managed solution (select all that apply)?

    1.   Managed solutions are exported as a RAR file

    2.   Managed solutions can never be customized further

    3.   Managed solutions can be exported

    4.   Managed solutions can be deleted

    5.   Managed solutions can be removed

Q. 4   What will happen when you try to export a solution that contains a claim custom entity that has a dependency on a policy custom entity without including the policy entity in your solution?

1. The solution export wizard will fail.

2. The solution export wizard will warn you and provide an option to include the policy entity.

3. The solution export wizard will automatically include the policy entity.

4. The solution will be successfully exported, but will fail if you try to import the solution into another CRM organization that does not contain the policy entity.

Q. 5   You have installed a new managed solution into your CRM organization, but one of the field label customizations on a form has not taken effect. This is most likely because:

1. You have installed a number of solutions in the wrong order.

2. CRM uses a top wins conflict resolution strategy for user interface customizations.

3. CRM uses a merge conflict resolution strategy for managed solutions.

4. The field label customizations on forms in managed solutions are resolved in favor of conflicting customizations in unmanaged solutions.

5. You did not choose the overwrite customizations option when importing your solution which would have overwritten any unmanaged customizations in place on components in your solution.

9
Sample Certification Exam Questions

This chapter provides 75 sample questions similar to those you can expect to find in the MB2-866 Microsoft Dynamics CRM 2011 Configuration and Customization exam. You should aim to complete all these questions within two hours. Answers are provided in Appendix B.

Q. 1

Your Microsoft Dynamics CRM 2011 organization includes one business unit and two custom entities called Publications and Authors. Publications can have many authors. Now, you have created a one-to-many relationship between them.

Your users need to be able to associate any author record with any parent publication record. The users already have a custom security role that grants them Create, Read, and Write privileges for the Author and Publication entities at the Organization level.

Which one of the following options describes the minimum additional security privileges needed to meet the requirement?

1. Do nothing. The current privileges are sufficient.
2. The Append and Append To privileges at the User level on the Author entity.
3. The Append and Append To privileges at the User level on the Publication entity.
4. The Append privilege at the Organization level on the Author entity and Append To privileges at the Organization level on the Publication entity.
5. The Append and Append To privileges at the Organization level on the Author and Publication entities.

Q. 2

You no longer need one of the business units in your Microsoft Dynamics CRM 2011 organization structure.

What is the correct procedure to delete the business unit?

1. Disable any child business units, disable any users assigned to the business unit, disable the business unit, and delete the business unit.
2. Reassign any child business units, reassign any users assigned to the business unit, reassign any teams assigned to the business unit, and then delete the business unit.
3. Delete any child business units, reassign any users assigned to the business unit, reassign any teams assigned to the business unit, disable the business unit, and then delete the business unit.
4. Reassign any child business units, reassign any users assigned to the business unit, reassign any teams assigned to the business unit, disable the business unit, and then delete the business unit.
5. Disable any child business units, disable any users assigned to the business unit, disable any teams assigned to the business unit, disable the business unit, and then delete the business unit.

Q. 3

You are explaining the difference between the entity-based security privileges and the task-based security privileges to a colleague.

Which of the following security privileges are the task-based security privileges with just two access levels (choose the correct two options)?

1. Override Invoice Pricing
2. View Audit History
3. Assign Account
4. Append Activity
5. Bulk Edit

Q. 4

Your organization has a Microsoft Dynamics CRM 2011 deployment with a root parent business unit called Global and two subsidiary business units called North and South. The North business unit has two further subsidiary business units called North East and North West. Currently, there are users assigned to each of the business units.

Your organization plans to merge the North and South offices into a single office, and you have been instructed to disable the North business unit.

What effect will this have (select all that apply)?

1. The users assigned to the North business unit will not be able to log on.
2. The users assigned to the North East business unit will not be able to log on.
3. The North East business unit will also be disabled.
4. The North East business unit will be reassigned to the Global business unit.
5. The users in the North East business unit will be able to log on.

Q. 5

You have been asked to create a new user record and assign a custom security role to the user's CRM user account.

You navigate to the Users area and click on New to launch a new user form.

Which of the following statements is/are true (select all that apply)?

1. You must add one of the standard security roles to the CRM user account before you can add a custom security role.
2. You must add the CRM user account to a team that has the custom security role assigned to it.
3. You must save the CRM user account before you can add the custom security role to it.
4. A user account must be created in Active Directory before a CRM user account can be created.
5. A user account will automatically be created in Active Directory, when you create the CRM user account.

Q. 6

You have been asked to add 120 new users to an on-premise Microsoft Dynamics CRM 2011 deployment at short notice. The Active Directory user accounts have already been created. The new users need to be created with different business units, custom security roles, access types, and licenses.

Which of the following statements is/are true (select all that apply)?

1. You can use the Multiple New Users wizard to add all the new users in a single batch.
2. You can use the Multiple New Users wizard to add the users in batches where the users' business unit, security roles, access types, and licenses are the same in each batch.
3. You cannot use the Multiple New Users wizard to create users that require custom security roles.
4. You cannot use the Multiple New Users wizard to assign users to teams.
5. You cannot use the Multiple New Users wizard if the users' Active Directory accounts exist in another domain.

Q. 7

In a Microsoft Dynamics CRM 2011 organization, a custom user-owned entity called Editorial Approval has been created. You have asked to update the Author custom security role so that authors can view any editorial approval record, but authors cannot create editorial approval records owned by other authors.

How should you configure the Author security role (select two)?

1. Configure the Read Editorial Approval privilege with Organization-level access.
2. Configure the Read Editorial Approval privilege with User-level access.
3. Configure the Create Editorial Approval privilege with Organization-level access.
4. Configure the Create Editorial Approval privilege with User-level access.
5. Configure the Create Editorial Approval privilege with None-level access.

Q. 8

In a Microsoft Dynamics CRM 2011 organization, security roles have been configured so that users can only view records in their own business unit.

You have added the Share privilege at the Organization access level to the security role of users with a security role in one of the business units.

Which one of the following statements best describes how the users will be able to share the records?

1. Users will be able to share records with users in their own business unit.

2. Users will be able to share records with teams in their own business unit.

3. Users will be able to share records with users and teams in their own business unit.

4. Users will be able to share records with users and teams in any business unit.

5. Users will be able to share records with any business unit.

Q. 9

A Microsoft Dynamics CRM 2011 implementation includes a custom team. The team is no longer required and you have been asked to delete it.

Select the option/options that best describes what you must do before you can delete the custom team (select all that apply).

1. If the team has members, the members must be removed.
2. If the team has security roles, the security roles must be removed.
3. If the team has field security profiles, the field security profiles must be removed.
4. If the team owns records, the records must be deleted.
5. If the team owns records, the records must be reassigned.

Q. 10

You have created a new CRM user account and assigned a custom security role for a new user.

Which one of the following alternatives would you have used to provide the user with the same privileges?

1. Assign the user to a business unit that had the custom security role assigned to it.
2. Assign the user to a manager that had been granted the custom security role.
3. Clone the CRM user account of another user that had been granted the custom security role.
4. Add the user to a field security profile that had the custom security role assigned to it.
5. Add the user to a team that had the custom security role assigned to it.

Q. 11

Business units A and B are both child business units of the root parent business units in a Microsoft Dynamics CRM 2011 organization. A custom security role has been created in business unit A.

Which option can be used to meet the custom security role from business unit A to business unit B?

1. Promote the custom security role to the root parent business unit and it will then be inherited by all child business units.
2. Copy the custom security role to the business unit B.
3. Create a new custom security role in the business unit B.
4. Export the custom security role from the business unit A and import it into the business unit B.
5. It is not possible for two business units to have security roles with the same name.

Q. 12

A CRM user has recently moved departments. You have updated the user's CRM user account by changing the user's manager and business unit. The user is unable to log in to the CRM system.

Choose the option that represents the most likely reason why the user is unable to log in to Microsoft Dynamics CRM.

1. The user's CRM user account does not have a security role assigned to it.
2. The user's new manager has not accepted the user into the new business unit.
3. The user's password has been reset.
4. The user's user account does not have a client access license associated with it.
5. The user does not own any CRM records.

Q. 13

You are unable to set the access level for the security privileges on a custom entity to the user, business unit, or parent: child business unit levels. The only access levels available are none and organization.

Which one of the following options is the most likely explanation?

1. Your security roles do not grant you sufficient privileges to set the access level to user, business unit, or parent: child business unit levels.

2. The custom entity is organization-owned.

3. The custom entity is user-owned.

4. The custom security role is assigned to the root parent business unit.

5. Auditing is not enabled for the custom entity.

Q. 14

A user was temporarily added to a team while a regular team member was on leave. A custom security role assigned to the team granted the user sufficient privileges to work with sales opportunities. Now that the user has been removed from the team, he/she no longer has any security privileges to work with opportunities.

Which option best describes what will happen to the opportunities that were owned by the user while he/she was temporarily a member of the team?

1. The opportunities will be reassigned to the team.

2. The opportunities will be reassigned to the team's administrator.

3. The opportunities will be reassigned to the user's manager.

4. The opportunities will be reassigned to the system administrator.

5. Nothing will happen to the opportunities owned by the user.

Q. 15

Which of the following constraints apply to assigning each CRM user to a manager (select all that apply)?

1. The manager must be in the same business unit as the user, or in a parental business unit to the user's business unit.

2. The manager must not be assigned to a child business unit of the user's business unit.

3. The manager's user account must be enabled.

4. The manager must have at least one security role.

5. The manager's user record must have a manager assigned.

Q. 16

A form for a custom entity currently displays the following links: Activities, Closed Activities, Connections, Documents, and Audit History.

Which of these links can be removed by modifying the options on the Entity Options section of the entity screen (select one)?

1. Activities and Closed Activities
2. Connections
3. Documents
4. Audit History
5. None of these links can be removed by modifying the options in the Entity Options section of the entity screen

Q. 17

Users have reported that no results are returned when they search on the values of an option set field by using the Quick Find feature.

What is the cause of this defect?

1. It is not possible to search for records using an option set value with the Quick Find feature.
2. You have not created a Quick Find view for the entity.
3. You have not configured any find columns in the Quick Find view.
4. Users need to use a wildcard character when using the Quick Find feature.
5. You have not configured any find columns in the Lookup view.

Q. 18

You have created a user-owned custom entity and later discovered that the entity should be organization-owned.

What is the correct procedure to achieve this?

1. Use the Change Entity Ownership feature on the entity form.
2. Use the Convert Entity Ownership feature on the solution components action toolbar.
3. Export the solution as unmanaged, edit the <OwnershipTypeMask> property in the customizations.xml file, and reimport the solution.
4. Export the solution as unmanaged, delete the <OwnerId>, <OwnerIdType>, and <OwnerIdName> attributes in the customizations.xml file, and reimport the solution.
5. Delete the user-owned custom entity and create a new organization-owned custom entity.

Q. 19

Which of the following statements about the managed properties of an entity are true (choose two)?

1. There are no supported methods for customizing an entity that is part of an unmanaged solution and its Can be customized property is False.
2. There are no supported methods for customizing an entity that is part of a managed solution and the Can be customized property is False.
3. You cannot modify the Can be customized property of system entities.
4. You can only modify an entity's managed properties, when it is in a managed solution.
5. Entities are the only components that have a Can be deleted managed property.

Q. 20

Which of the following facts regarding the field-level security are true?

1. Field-level security applies to data displayed in the results of an Advanced Find query.
2. Field-level security applies to data displayed in reports.
3. Field-level security applies to data displayed in reports that are exported to a PDF document and given to a CRM user that does have the appropriate field security profile.
4. Field-level security applies to data displayed in reports that are exported to an Excel workbook and given to a person that does use Microsoft Dynamics CRM.
5. Field-level security can be applied to any system field.

Q. 21

Which of the following statements regarding fields is true?

1. An option set component can be used by more than one entity.
2. A two options field can be used by two entities.
3. The values of the Status Reason fields can be modified.
4. The values of the Status fields can be modified.
5. A whole number field can be used by more than one entity when the Duration field format is used.

Q. 22

In a Microsoft Dynamics CRM 2011 organization, the Phone Number field on the account entity has a requirement level of Business Required.

What are the potential sources of records that have a missing phone number?

1. Users might have deleted the phone number when saving accounts.
2. Users might have used CRM for Outlook to synchronize the CRM account records with Outlook account records that do not have a phone number.
3. A user might have imported account records with no phone number by using the Data Import Wizard.
4. The enterprise resource planning system, which creates accounts in CRM through a one-way integration by using the CRM web service, might have created accounts with no phone number.
5. Users may have ignored the warning about the missing phone number when saving new account records.

Q. 23

What are the differences between an option set field created within an entity and a global option set created within a solution (choose two)?

1. When you add a new value to a global option set, the new value appears in all option set fields using the global option set.
2. When you change the default value of a global option set, the new default value applies to all option set fields using the global option set.
3. When you enable auditing for a global option set, auditing is enabled for all option set fields using the global option set.
4. When you set the requirement level for a global option set, the requirement level applies to all option set fields using the global option set.
5. You cannot delete a global option set that is used by an option set field.

Q. 24

You are about to configure the options in the System Settings pop-up window.

Which of the following settings can be managed in the System Settings area (select all that apply)?

1. The default number of rows per page displayed in system views.
2. The currency precision used for pricing throughout the system.

3. The organizational standards—such as number, currency, time, and date formats—applied to new users.

4. The organizational standards—such as number, currency, time, and date formats—applied to existing users.

5. Contact, task, and appointment synchronization options for CRM for Outlook users.

Q. 25

Which one of the following procedures describes the correct process for deleting a custom entity?

1. Open your unmanaged development solution, select the entity in the entity components list, and click on the Delete button in the solution actions toolbar.

2. In the Customizations area, click on Customize the System, select the custom entity, and click on Remove in the actions toolbar of the default solution.

3. In the Customizations area, click on Delete Entity and follow the steps in the Entity Deletion Wizard.

4. Publish your development solution as a managed solution, delete the custom entity from the customizations.xml file within the solution package, and reimport the solution file.

Q. 26

You have been asked to customize the user interface of Microsoft Dynamics CRM 2011.

Which of the following statements are true (choose two)?

1. Custom buttons can be added to the ribbon for most forms.

2. SiteMap can be customized by using the drag-and-drop SiteMap designer.

3. The display order of navigation items in the left-hand navigation area of most forms can be customized.

4. Custom JavaScript is required to control the visibility of the Form Assistant on the Case form.

5. Microsoft Dynamics CRM 2011 includes a new Dependent Option Sets feature.

Q. 27

You have created a custom activity entity, entity calls and you have been asked to modify the system so that only sales people can view sales calls.

Which one of the following statements is true?

1. Custom activity entities can be organization-owned.
2. Custom activity entities can be displayed in the main application left-hand navigation pane by checking the appropriate option in the Areas that display this entity section on the custom entity form.
3. Custom activity entities cannot be audited.
4. Security roles provide the same privileges to all system activity and custom activity entities.
5. Custom activity entities can be synchronized as Outlook tasks by using Microsoft Dynamics CRM for Outlook.

Q. 28

In which of the following areas will new custom fields be available to users before the solution is published (choose two)?

1. In system views
2. In system charts
3. In personal views using Advanced Find
4. In reports using the Report Wizard
5. On forms

Q. 29

You have been asked to delete an unmanaged solution from a development organization. The solution contains custom entities and system entities.

Choose all the steps that you must follow to dispose of the solution and its components.

1. Remove the custom entities
2. Remove the system entities
3. Delete the custom entities
4. Delete the system entities
5. Delete the solution record

Q. 30

Which of the following statements regarding field datatypes are true (choose all that apply)?

1. Calculated Number fields enable customizers to store the results of simple arithmetic calculations in a field.

2. Date and Time fields cannot be used to store dates prior to January 1, 1990.

3. Lookup fields can be created from the form designer to quickly create new 1:N entity relationships.

4. Multiple Option Set fields enable users to select one or more values from a pre-defined list of options.

5. Single Line of Text fields can store up to 4,000 characters, but once saved the length cannot be changed.

Q. 31

Which of the following statements about entity relationships in Microsoft Dynamics CRM 2011 are true (choose two)?

1. self-referential relationships are not possible.

2. True one-to-one relationships are only available with custom development.

3. custom polymorphic relationships are a standard feature.

4. Two types of many-to-many relationships are possible.

5. customizable intersection entities are a feature of both 1:N and N:1 relationships.

Q. 32

When a new record B is created, some field values from the parent record A should be copied onto record B automatically.

Which one of the following features will achieve this requirement?

1. Configure a Cascade All relationship rule between the A and B entities.

2. Configure a dialog process to copy the appropriate field values from record A to record B after record B is saved.

3. Develop a database trigger to copy the appropriate field values from record A to record B.

4. Schedule the Bulk Edit procedure to copy the appropriate field values from the parent records to the child records.

5. Configure relationship field mappings between the appropriate fields on A and B entities, then create a new B record from parent record A.

Q. 33

A custom 1:N relationship has been created between the Contact system entity and a custom entity. The relationship behavior specified is Configurable Cascading.

Which of the following options correctly describe/describes the actions for you to configure the relationship behavior (select all that apply)?

1. Activate
2. Assign
3. Deactivate
4. Delete
5. Unshare

Q. 34

When a user deletes an account record, the related opportunities are also deleted.

Which of the following relationship behaviors do you need to explain to the user (select two)?

1. Remove Link
2. Cascade All
3. Parental
4. Referential, Restrict Delete
5. Cascade None

Q. 35

A custom entity, Like, has been created in your organization. A contact can have zero or more likes and a like can apply to zero or more contacts. No other attributes about *likes* are needed.

Which one of the following entity relationships should you create to meet this requirement?

1. 1:N self-referential relationship between contacts and likes
2. N:1 relationship between likes and contacts
3. Native N:N relationship between likes and contacts
4. Manual N:N relationship between likes and contacts
5. 1:N relationship between likes and contacts

Q. 36

You have configured some entity relationship field mappings on the 1:N relationship between accounts and cases.

What are the limitations of entity field mappings that users should be aware of (select two)?

1. An error message will pop-up if the customer of a case is a contact and not an account.
2. If the values of the mapped fields of the account record are modified after the case has been created, the values of the mapped fields of the account's associated cases will also be modified.
3. If the values of the mapped fields of the account record are modified after the case has been created, the values of the mapped fields of the associated cases will not be modified.
4. If the values of the mapped fields of the case record are modified, the values of the mapped fields of the associated account will also be modified.
5. If a case is created from the New button on the ribbon of the Cases grid, the values from an account specified in the Customer lookup field will not be mapped to the case.

Q. 37

You have configured some entity relationship field mappings on the 1:N relationship between accounts and cases.

What are the technical restrictions that apply to entity field mapping (select two)?

1. Target fields can only be mapped to a single source field
2. Target fields cannot be mapped, if they are read-only on a form
3. Option set field values must be manually mapped
4. Text fields must be of equal length before they can be mapped
5. Fields must be of the same datatype before they can be mapped

Q. 38

As well as specifying a connected record and a connection role, what other attributes are users able to store in a connection record (select one)?

1. Description, Start Date, and End Date
2. Description, Start Date, End Date, and Owner
3. Description, Start Date, End Date, Owner, and Status Reason
4. Description, and Status Reason
5. Description

Q. 39

Which of the following statements regarding self-referential relationships are false (choose two)?

1. Self-referential relationships can only be used for representing parental relationships
2. Self-referential relationships cannot be used to create a circular relationship between records
3. Self-referential relationships can have a parental behavior
4. Many-to-many self-referential relationships are not supported
5. Self-referential relationships support entity relationship field mapping

Q. 40

Which of the following user interface components cannot be added to a form using the standard user interface customization capabilities of Microsoft Dynamics CRM 2011 (choose two)?

1. Tabs
2. Sub-grid charts
3. Silverlight controls
4. Sub-forms
5. Sub-grids with inline editing

Q. 41

Which one of the following customizations should you perform so that only contacts associated with the account through the Parent Customer field on the contact record can be selected as the Primary Contact for the account?

1. Disable the Display Search Box in lookup dialog option on the Primary Contact field on the account form.
2. Enable Related record filtering on the Parent Customer field on the contact form.
3. Enable Related record filtering on the Primary Contact field on the account form.
4. Enable Related record filtering on the Primary Contact field on the account form and the Parent Customer field on the contact form.
5. Enable the Turn off automatic resolutions in the field option on the Primary Contact field on the account form.

Q. 42

You have added some custom fields to the standard form for the account entity in a solution in your development organization and exported your solution as a managed solution. An earlier version of the same solution in an unmanaged state was previously imported into your test organization. You are about to import the latest version of the managed solution into your test organization.

Which of the following steps describe how to correctly have your custom fields displayed on the account form in your test organization (select all that apply)?

1. Delete the earlier version of the managed solution.
2. Import the managed solution by selecting the Maintain customizations (recommended) option during the import procedure.
3. Import the managed solution by selecting the Overwrite customizations option during the import procedure.
4. Download the log file at the end of the import procedure.
5. Publish all customizations.

Q. 43

You need to change the parent business unit of an existing business unit.

Which of the following statements is true when a child business unit's parent business unit is changed?

1. All the child business unit's users and teams move with it.
2. All the users in the child business unit are deactivated.
3. The security roles are removed from all the users in the child business unit. New security roles need to be specified for each user.

4. Circular relationships between business units are supported where required, but not recommended.

5. There is a constraint of seven levels in the organization hierarchy, excluding the root parent business unit.

Q. 44

Which of the following properties of a custom view can not be customized through the standard Microsoft Dynamics CRM 2011 view customization features (select two)?

1. Records per page
2. Filter criteria
3. Primary and secondary sort columns
4. View name
5. Conditional row formatting

Q. 45

You have created a custom field for a system entity, but you have not yet added the field to a form or view.

Which of the following properties of your custom field can not be modified by using the standard Microsoft Dynamics CRM 2011 field customization features (select two)?

1. Field security
2. Auditing
3. Name
4. Display name
5. Type

Q. 46

You need to move a business unit and all the records it owns to a new position in the organization hierarchy.

Which one of the following statements describes what you should do?

1. Delete the business unit and recreate it under the correct business unit.
2. Deactivate the business unit, delete it, and then recreate it under the correct business unit.
3. Drag the business unit to the correct position in the organization hierarchy.

4. Use the Change Parent Business feature in the Business Units grid action menu.

5. Create a new business unit, move all the users from the old business unit to the new business unit, and then delete the old business unit.

Q. 47

You need to add a chart to the account form showing the value of won sales opportunities each month in columns.

You have opened the account form editor. What steps do you need to take to add the chart to the account form (choose all that apply)?

1. Click on the Sub-Grid button from the Insert tab.

2. Click on the Chart button from the Insert tab.

3. In the Data Source section of the List or Chart Properties window, select Opportunities (Potential Customer) as the Entity and Closed Opportunities as the Default View.

4. In the Chart Option section of the List or Chart Properties window, select Actual Revenue by Month as the Default Chart.

5. In the Chart Option section of the List or Chart Properties window, select Column as the Chart Type.

Q. 48

Which one of the following Microsoft Dynamics CRM 2011 features can be used to restrict access to the data stored in a custom field on a system entity?

1. Security roles

2. Field-level security

3. Database encryption

4. Role-based forms

5. Security privileges

Q. 49

Which of the following statements regarding the root parent business unit is/are true (select all that apply)?

1. The organization's display name can be modified.

2. The root parent business unit's name can be modified.

3. The root parent business unit can be re-parented.

4. The root parent business unit can be deleted.

5. The root parent business unit can be deactivated.

Q. 50

Which one of the following methods would you use so that members of a custom team can use a user's personal view, but it cannot be seen by other users?

1. Instruct the user to share his personal view with the custom team.

2. Create the user's view as a public view and share it with the custom team.

3. Convert the user's personal view into a team view.

4. Inform the user that it is not possible to share his view with the custom team.

5. Instruct the user to export his personal view, then import it as a system view.

Q. 51

You have created a public view on the account entity called Large Customer Accounts, which includes a filter criterion for records where the Customer Size equals Large. Customer Size is an option set with the options—Small, Medium, and Large.

Which one of the following methods would you use to create two more views, Small Customer Accounts and Medium Customer Accounts, with the same columns and sort order as the Large Customer Accounts view, but filter records where the Customer Size equals Small and Medium, respectively?

1. Use the Copy View feature to create two copies of the Large Customer Accounts view, and then modify the name and filter criteria of each of the copies.

2. Modify the filter criteria of the Large Customer Accounts view so that it includes accounts where the Customer Size equals Small, Medium, or Large.

3. Manually create a new account view with a filter for accounts where the Customer Size equals Medium and create a secondary filter criteria for accounts where the Customer Size is Small.

4. Modify the Large Customer Accounts view to include a second filter criteria for accounts where the Customer Size equals Medium and third filter criteria for accounts where the Customer Size is Small.

5. Use the Save As feature to create two copies of the Large Customer Accounts view, and then modify the name and filter criteria of each of the copies.

Q. 52

A user with the Sales Manager security role in business unit B has created a chart.

Which one of the following options best describes how the user can share the chart with other users in business unit B without sharing the chart with users in other business units?

1. The user should export her user chart and reimport it as a system chart.
2. The user should export her user chart and you can import it as a system chart because you have a System Administrator security role.
3. The user should export her chart and you can import it as a system chart because you have a System Administrator security role, then you can configure which business units can use the chart.
4. The user should share her user chart with the business unit B's team.
5. It's not possible to share a user chart.

Q. 53

Which two of the following statements correctly describe the differences between the managed and unmanaged solutions?

1. You cannot create a new unmanaged solution in an organization.
2. You cannot create a new managed solution in an organization.
3. You cannot add solution components to a managed solution.
4. You cannot export an unmanaged solution from an organization.
5. You cannot export a managed solution from an organization.

Q. 54

You need to create a new mobile form for a custom entity. When you create a new mobile form which fields will be already displayed on the form?

1. All fields where the datatype is Lookup.
2. The Name, Owner, and Status fields.
3. All fields where the requirement level is Business Required.
4. All system fields displayed on the published fallback form.
5. No fields will be displayed by default on the new mobile form.

Q. 55

A one-to-many relationship has been created between two custom entities, policies and claims. The main policy form should display all claims that are related to the policy. Inactive claims that have been settled should be displayed in addition to active claims that are currently being processed.

How would you customize the system to meet this requirement (select one)?

1. It is not possible to meet this requirement without custom development.
2. The Claims link in the left-hand navigation area of the Policy form will display the Claims Associated View which includes all associated claims by default. No customization is necessary.
3. Add a sub-grid to the policy form. Configure the sub-grid to display active and inactive claims associated with the policy.
4. Add an iFrame to the policy form. Configure the iFrame to display active and inactive claims associated with the policy.
5. Add a view to the policy form. Configure the view to display active and inactive claims associated with the policy.

Q. 56

Which one of the following statements describes what will be deleted when you delete an unmanaged solution?

1. All the entities in the solution
2. All the custom entities in the solution
3. All the custom entities in the solution, unless they are dependent components from another unmanaged solution
4. All the custom entities in the solution, unless they are referenced components from another solution
5. Nothing else would be deleted

Q. 57

A managed solution containing a custom entity has been exported from a source organization and imported into a target organization for testing. Several fields that should be included in the entity are missing.

What would you do to add the missing fields to the custom entity in the target organization (choose one)?

1. Set the Can be customized property of the managed solution in the test CRM system to True and then add the missing fields.

2. Modify the Can be customized property of the custom entity in the managed solution in test CRM system to True and then add the missing fields.
3. Add the missing fields to the custom entity in the unmanaged solution in the development CRM system, export it as a managed solution, and import it into the test CRM system.
4. Add the missing fields to the custom entity in the managed solution in the test CRM system.
5. Delete the managed solution from the test CRM system, modify the XML of the managed solution file, and import it into the test CRM system.

Q. 58

Which of the following statements regarding charts are true (choose all that apply)?

1. Charts can be displayed on a dashboard.
2. Charts can be launched from the Charts link in the My Work group in the Workplace area of the main application screen.
3. Charts can be displayed in a grid associated with the selected view.
4. Charts can be displayed in a sub-grid component on a form.
5. Chart visibility can be restricted based on the chart owner and business unit.

Q. 59

Which of the following statements regarding chart types is true?

1. The standard chart types are drilldown, column, line, and pie charts.
2. The standard chart types are column, bar, line, pie, and funnel charts.
3. The standard chart types are area, point, pyramid, range, and doughnut charts.
4. Other chart types can be used by exporting the chart, customizing the chart XML, and re-importing the chart.
5. A System Administrator or System Customizer security role is required to change the chart type of system charts.

Q. 60

Which of the following statements about role-based forms is true (select all that apply)?

1. By default, only users with a System Administrator or System Customizer security role have access to a new form.
2. By default, all users have access to all custom forms.
3. Security roles can be used to control access to entity-based or task-based privileges, but not forms.
4. A field-security profile is required for each form.
5. At least one form for each entity must be specified as the fallback form.

Q. 61

Which of the following steps are required to configure auditing in Microsoft Dynamics CRM 2011 (select all that apply)?

1. Configure deployment-level auditing in CRM Deployment Manager.
2. Configure database-level auditing in Microsoft SQL Server.
3. Configure organization-level auditing in global audit settings.
4. Configure entity-level auditing for each entity that must be audited.
5. Configure field-level auditing for each field that must be audited.

Q. 62

Which of the following statements best describes the auditing features of Microsoft Dynamics CRM 2011 (choose all that apply)?

1. Auditing is not enabled by default.
2. Only custom fields on system or custom entities can be audited.
3. Only system fields on system or custom entities can be audited.
4. The only entities that can be audited are the Common entities, Sales entities, Marketing entities, and Customer Service entities.
5. Only custom entities can be audited.

Q. 63

Which of the following statements correctly describe the standard auditing function of Microsoft Dynamics CRM 2011 (select two)?

1. An audit record is created when a user runs a report.
2. An audit record is created when a user runs a query by using Advanced Find.

3. An audit record is created when a user deletes a customer record.
4. Advanced Find cannot be used to query the audit data for specific events.
5. Users can delete audit records.

Q. 64

During routine maintenance of the Microsoft Dynamics CRM 2011 database, you notice that the audit logs are consuming a significant amount of space on the database server.

Which of the following actions are supported by Microsoft Dynamics CRM 2011 (choose all that apply)?

1. The audit log can be shrunk to reduce its size.
2. Any audit log can be exported to a file.
3. Any audit log can be deleted.
4. Only the oldest audit log can be deleted.
5. Only the most recent audit log can be exported to a file.

Q. 65

Which one of the following actions could you take to compile a list of all the records deleted from the CRM system over the past 12 months?

1. Use the Audit History View for deleted records.
2. Use the Audit Summary View to filter for deletion events.
3. Use Advanced Find and export audit deletion events to Excel.
4. Develop a custom report list of deleted records by querying the Audit Filtered Views.
5. Back up the database audit partitions.

Q. 66

A user has reported that no audit records are displayed in the Audit History View on records of a custom entity.

What are the possible causes of this issue (select two)?

1. The audit log is full.
2. Auditing has not been started at the organization level.
3. User access auditing has not been enabled for the organization.

4. The user's security role does not have sufficient privileges to view audit records.

5. No fields on the custom entity have been configured for auditing.

Q. 67

Which of the following statements about the default solution are true (select two)?

1. The default solution can be exported as a managed solution.
2. The default solution can be deleted.
3. The default solution contains solution components imported from unmanaged solutions.
4. The display name of the default solution can be modified.
5. The default solution can be exported as an unmanaged solution.

Q. 68

When setting up a new CRM organization, you need to set up a new publisher.

Which of the following are fields on the publisher record (select all that apply)?

1. Name
2. Microsoft Partner Network membership number
3. Prefix
4. Suffix
5. Version

Q. 69

The solution import procedure fails and you need to troubleshoot the cause of the error.

Which one of the following statements is true?

1. The cause of the solution import failure will be automatically reported to the Microsoft partner for root cause analysis.
2. The cause of the solution import failure will be recorded in the solution import log file.
3. The cause of the solution import failure will only be logged, if you have enabled tracing on the CRM server.
4. The cause of the solution import failure cannot be logged.

5. The cause of the solution import failure will be displayed in the solution's configuration page.

Q. 70

Accidentally, you have deleted your CRM development organization and you want to use a managed solution file from your testing organization to restore a new CRM development organization.

Which one of the following statements is true?

1. It is possible to export a managed solution as an unmanaged solution only if you have enabled the solution's Can be customized property before you export it.
2. You can export the managed solution from the CRM testing organization as an unmanaged solution and import it into your new CRM development organization.
3. There is no supported method for converting a managed solution to an unmanaged solution.
4. You can reference the managed solution's components in a new unmanaged solution and export the unmanaged solution from your testing organization.
5. You can convert the managed solution to an unmanaged solution by combining it with an unmanaged solution by using the merge conflict resolution strategy.

Q. 71

You are promoting your customizations by exporting a solution from your CRM development organization and importing it into the CRM test organization.

Which of the following can be included in the exported solution (select all that apply)?

1. Business units
2. Outlook synchronization settings
3. Workflow processes
4. Teams
5. Auditing settings

Q. 72

You no longer need a custom entity in your unmanaged solution A. The entity was created in unmanaged solution B and added to solution A.

Which of the following statements is/are true (select all that apply)?

1. If you remove the entity from solution A, it will be removed from solution B.
2. If you delete the entity from solution A, it will be deleted from solution B.
3. If you delete the entity from solution A, all records of the entity will be deleted.
4. If you remove the entity from solution A, all records of the entity will be deleted.
5. If you delete solution A, the entity will be deleted.

Q. 73

Which of the following statements correctly describes the differences between a managed solution and an unmanaged solution (select all that apply)?

1. Managed solutions can be exported, but unmanaged solutions cannot be exported.
2. New solution components cannot be added to the managed solutions, but can be added to the unmanaged solutions.
3. Customization conflicts in the user interface components are resolved in favor of unmanaged solutions.
4. Customization conflicts, except for those in user interface components, are resolved in favor of managed solutions.
5. Solution components from a managed solution can be added to another unmanaged solution, but solution components from an unmanaged solution cannot be added to another unmanaged solution.

Q. 74

Which of the following are managed properties for custom entities that you can configure (select all that apply)?

1. New views can be created.
2. New fields can be created.
3. Schema name can be modified.
4. Display name can be modified.
5. Entity can be deleted.

Q. 75

In your development system, you decide to delete an unmanaged solution that contains several system and custom entities.

Which of the following steps would you take to delete the solution and its entities (choose all that apply)?

1. Export the solution as a managed solution and then delete it.
2. Remove the custom entities.
3. Delete the custom entities.
4. Delete the system entities.
5. Delete the unmanaged solution.

Answers to Sample Certification Exam Questions

This appendix provides the answers to the sample exam questions posed in *Chapter 9*, *Sample Certification Exam Questions*.

How much did you score?

Q. 1

1. Incorrect. The current privileges are not sufficient because Create, Read, and Write privileges do not enable records to be associated.

2. Incorrect. The Append To privilege on the Author entity is not required. The user-level privileges are insufficient to associate any author and publication records, and the Append To privilege on the Publication entity is also required.

3. Incorrect. Append privilege on the Publication entity is not required; User-level privileges are insufficient to associate any author and publication records; and Append privilege on the Author entity is also required.

4. Correct.

5. Incorrect. The question is asked for the minimum security privileges, but the Append To privilege on the Author entity is not required and the Append privilege on the Publication entity is not required.

Q. 2

1. Incorrect. The child business units need to be reassigned first, and the business unit must be disabled before it can be deleted.

2. Incorrect. The business unit must be disabled before it can be deleted.

3. Incorrect. The child business units should not be deleted.

4. Correct.

5. Incorrect. The child business units, users, and teams must be reassigned, not disabled, before the business unit can be deleted.

Q. 3

1. Incorrect. Override Invoice Pricing is a task-based privilege, but has five access levels.

2. Correct.

3. Incorrect. Assign Account is an entity-based privilege.

4. Incorrect. Append Activity is an entity-based privilege.

5. Correct.

Q. 4

1. Correct.

2. Correct.

3. Correct.

4. Incorrect. Disabling a business unit does not cause its child business units to be reassigned.

5. Incorrect. The North East business unit will also be disabled, so users assigned to this business unit will not be able to log in.

Q. 5

1. Incorrect. Using the standard security roles is optional.

2. Incorrect. Using teams is optional.

3. Correct.

4. Correct.

5. Incorrect. An active user account must exist in Active Directory before a CRM user account can be created.

Q. 6

1. Incorrect. You can use the Multiple New Users wizard to add the users in batches where the users' business unit, security roles, access types and licenses are the same in each batch.

2. Correct.

3. Incorrect. Custom security roles can be assigned by using the Multiple New Users wizard.

4. Correct.

5. Incorrect. Users can be added from any trusted Active Directory domain.

Q. 7

1. Correct.

2. Incorrect. A user-level read privilege would prevent authors from viewing editorial approvals unless they own the record.

3. Incorrect. An organization-level create privilege would enable authors to create editorial approvals owned by any user.

4. Correct.

5. Incorrect. A none-level create privilege would prevent authors from creating editorial approval records.

Q. 8

1. Incorrect. Fundraising users will be able to share records with users and teams in any business unit.

2. Incorrect. Fundraising users will be able to share records with users and teams in any business unit.

3. Incorrect. Fundraising users will be able to share records with users and teams in any business unit.

4. Correct.

5. Incorrect. Records cannot be shared directly with a business unit—can be shared only with users or teams.

Q. 9

1. Incorrect. Teams with members can be deleted.
2. Incorrect. Teams with security roles can be deleted.
3. Incorrect. Teams with the field security profiles can be deleted.
4. Incorrect. Teams that own records should have the records reassigned — not deleted — before the team is deleted.
5. Correct.

Q. 10

1. Incorrect. Security roles cannot be assigned to business units.
2. Incorrect. A user's security privileges are unrelated to the security roles of the user's manager.
3. Incorrect. There is no feature to clone a user.
4. Incorrect. Security roles cannot be assigned to field security profiles.
5. Correct.

Q. 11

1. Incorrect. There is no feature to promote a security role.
2. Incorrect. It is not possible to copy a security role to a different business unit.
3. Correct.
4. Incorrect. Business units cannot be exported and imported between organizations.
5. Incorrect. Two business units can have security roles with the same name.

Q. 12

1. Correct.
2. Incorrect. A manager does not need to accept a change in a user's business unit.
3. Incorrect. CRM does not store user passwords.
4. Incorrect. A client access license does not need to be associated with a CRM user account.
5. Incorrect. Users do not need to own records to log in.

Q. 13

1. Incorrect. If you had insufficient privileges, you would not be able to edit the custom security role at all.

2. Correct.

3. Incorrect. User- or team-owned entities have five access levels.

4. Incorrect. The business unit of the security role has no effect on the access levels.

5. Incorrect. Auditing of the custom entity has no effect on the access levels.

Q. 14

1. Incorrect. User's opportunities are not reassigned and remain owned by the user even though he/she has no privileges to work with opportunity records.

2. Incorrect. User's opportunities are not reassigned and remain owned by the user even though he/she has no privileges to work with opportunity records.

3. Incorrect. User's opportunities are not reassigned and remain owned by the user even though he/she has no privileges to work with opportunity records.

4. Incorrect. User's opportunities are not reassigned and remain owned by the user even though he/she has no privileges to work with opportunity records.

5. Correct.

Q. 15

1. Correct.

2. Correct.

3. Incorrect. The manager's user record can be disabled.

4. Incorrect. The manager's user record does not need to have a security role assigned.

5. Incorrect. The manager's user record does not need to have a manager assigned.

Q. 16

1. Incorrect. Activities cannot be disabled after they have been enabled for an entity.

2. Incorrect. Connections cannot be disabled after they have been enabled for an entity.

3. Correct.

4. Incorrect. The Audit History link can only be removed by modifying a user's View Audit History security privilege.

5. Incorrect. The Documents link can be removed.

Q. 17

1. Incorrect. It is possible to search by using option set fields with the Quick Find feature.

2. Incorrect. A Quick Find view is automatically created when you create a custom entity.

3. Correct.

4. Incorrect. A wildcard character is optional when using the Quick Find feature.

5. Incorrect. The find columns are not configured for Lookup Views.

Q. 18

1. Incorrect. There is no Change Entity Ownership feature.

2. Incorrect. There is no Convert Entity Ownership feature.

3. Incorrect. Editing the `customizations.xml` file is not supported.

4. Incorrect. Editing the `customizations.xml` file is not supported.

5. Correct.

Q. 19

1. Correct.

2. Incorrect. The display name can be modified.

3. Incorrect. The Field Security property can be modified for custom fields.

4. Incorrect. The Requirement Level can be modified.

5. Correct.

Q. 20

1. Correct.
2. Correct.
3. Incorrect. Data exported from a report to a PDF document can be viewed by anyone.
4. Incorrect: Data exported from a report to an Excel workbook can be viewed by anyone.
5. Incorrect: Field-level security can only be applied to custom fields and cannot be applied to system fields.

Q. 21

1. Correct.
2. Incorrect. A two options field can only be used by one entity.
3. Correct.
4. Incorrect. The values of the Status fields cannot be modified.
5. Incorrect. A whole number field can only be used by one entity regardless of the field format.

Q. 22

1. Incorrect. It is not possible to save a record that has a value missing from a field with a requirement level of Business Required.
2. Incorrect. CRM for Outlook does not synchronize account records between CRM and Outlook.
3. Correct.
4. Correct.
5. Incorrect. It is not possible to save a record that has a value missing from a field with a requirement level of Business Required.

Q. 23

1. Correct.
2. Incorrect. The global option set components do not have a default value.
3. Incorrect. The global option set components do not have an audit property.
4. Incorrect. The global option sets components do not have a requirement level property.
5. Correct.

Q. 24

1. Incorrect. This is a personal setting for each user.
2. Correct.
3. Correct.
4. Incorrect. The existing users are not affected by changes to the organizational standards system settings.
5. Incorrect. This is a personal setting for each user.

Q. 25

1. Incorrect. Removing a solution component does not delete the solution component.
2. Correct.
3. Incorrect. Removing a solution component does not delete the solution component and solution components cannot be removed from the default solution.
4. Incorrect. There is no Entity Deletion Wizard.
5. Incorrect. Deleting an entity from the `customizations.xml` does not delete an entity when the solution is imported into an organization.

Q. 26

1. Correct.
2. Incorrect. There is no drag-and-drop SiteMap designer.
3. Correct.
4. Incorrect. The case form includes an option to enable or disable the Form Assistant.
5. Incorrect. There is no Dependent Option Sets feature.

Q. 27

1. Incorrect. Custom activity entities cannot be organization-owned.
2. Incorrect. The Areas that display this entity section is read-only for the custom activity entities.
3. Incorrect. Custom activities can be audited.
4. Correct.
5. Incorrect. Custom activity entities do not synchronize with the Outlook tasks using Microsoft Dynamics CRM for Outlook.

Q. 28

1. Incorrect. System view modifications are not available until customizations are published.

2. Incorrect. System chart modifications are not available until customizations are published.

3. Correct.

4. Correct.

5. Incorrect. Form modifications are not available until customizations are published.

Q. 29

1. Incorrect. Removing the custom entities from the solution will not delete the custom entities from the default solution.

2. Correct.

3. Correct.

4. Incorrect. System entities cannot be deleted.

5. Correct.

Q. 30

1. Incorrect. There is no calculated number datatype.

2. Correct.

3. Correct.

4. Incorrect. There is no multiple option set datatype.

5. Incorrect. The length of a single line of text field can be modified.

Q. 31

1. Incorrect. Self-referential relationships are possible.

2. Correct.

3. Incorrect. Custom polymorphic relationships are not a standard feature.

4. Correct.

5. Incorrect. Customizable intersection entities is a feature of the N:N relationships.

Q. 32

1. Incorrect. Relationship rules do not copy the field values when records are created.

2. Incorrect. Dialog processes cannot be triggered after records are saved.

3. Incorrect. Database triggers are not possible.

4. Incorrect. The Bulk Edit feature cannot be used to copy field values from one record to records of a different entity.

5. Correct.

Q. 33

1. Incorrect. Activating a primary record is not a configurable relationship behavior.

2. Correct.

3. Incorrect. Deactivating a primary record is not a configurable relationship behavior.

4. Correct.

5. Correct.

Q. 34

1. Incorrect. The Remove Link cascading option would not explain why opportunities related to accounts are being deleted.

2. Correct.

3. Correct.

4. Incorrect. The Referential, Restrict Delete relationship behavior would not explain why opportunities related to accounts are being deleted.

5. Incorrect. The Cascade None cascading option would not explain why opportunities related to accounts are being deleted.

Q. 35

1. Incorrect. A self-referential relationship is created between an entity and itself — not between two different entities.

2. Incorrect. An N:1 relationship between interests and contacts would not enable interests to be associated with zero or more contacts.

3. Correct.

4. Incorrect. A manual N:N relationship is not required if no other attributes about contacts' interests are needed.

5. Incorrect. A 1:N relationship between interests and contacts would not enable contacts to be associated with zero or more interests.

Q. 36

1. Incorrect. No field values will be mapped and no error message will appear.

2. Incorrect. If fields in the primary record are later modified, changes are not cascaded down to related records.

3. Correct.

4. Incorrect. If fields in the related records are modified, the changes do not cascade up to the primary record.

5. Correct.

Q. 37

1. Correct.

2. Incorrect. The target fields can be read-only.

3. Incorrect. The option set field values are mapped automatically by using the integer values for each option.

4. Incorrect. The target field can be longer than the source field.

5. Correct.

Q. 38

1. Incorrect. The **Owner** can also be stored.

2. Correct.

3. Incorrect. Connection records do not have a Status Reason.

4. Incorrect. Connection records do not have a Status Reason.

5. Incorrect. The Start Date, End Date, and Owner can also be stored.

Q. 39

1. Correct.
2. Incorrect. Direct and indirect circular relationships between records are not allowed.
3. Incorrect. Self-referential relationships can have a parental behavior.
4. Correct.
5. Incorrect. Entity relationship field mapping is possible with the self-referential relationships.

Q. 40

1. Incorrect. Tabs are standard user interface components that can be added to forms.
2. Incorrect. Sub-grid charts are standard user interface components that can be added to forms.
3. Incorrect. Silverlight controls are standard web resources that can be added to forms.
4. Correct.
5. Correct.

Q. 41

1. Incorrect. Disabling the search box still enables users to browse and select contacts associated with other accounts.
2. Incorrect. The Parent Customer field on the contact form has no impact on the Primary Contact field on the account form.
3. Correct.
4. Incorrect. The Parent Customer field on the contact form has no impact on the Primary Contact field on the account form.
5. Incorrect. Enabling the Turn off automatic resolutions in the field option on the Primary Contact field on the account form has no impact on the records that the user can select.

Q. 42

1. Incorrect. Deleting the earlier versions of the managed solution is not necessary.
2. Incorrect. Selecting this option will cause new user interface customizations to remain invisible.

3. Correct.
4. Incorrect. This step is optional but not necessary.
5. Incorrect. This step is not necessary.

Q. 43

1. Correct.
2. Incorrect. The users are not deactivated.
3. Incorrect. The users' security roles are not removed.
4. Incorrect. The circular business unit relationships are blocked.
5. Incorrect. There is no constraint to the levels in the organization hierarchy.

Q. 44

1. Correct.
2. Incorrect. You can customize the filter criteria.
3. Incorrect. You can customize the primary and secondary sort options.
4. Incorrect. You can customize the view name.
5. Correct.

Q. 45

1. Incorrect. You can customize the field security of custom fields.
2. Incorrect. You can customize the auditing.
3. Correct.
4. Incorrect. You can customize the display name.
5. Correct.

Q. 46

1. Incorrect. Deleting a business unit will delete all records owned by the business unit (except users, teams, and child business units).
2. Incorrect. Deleting a business unit will delete all records owned by the business unit (except users, teams, and child business units).
3. Incorrect. There is no drag-and-drop feature for moving business units.
4. Correct.
5. Incorrect. This procedure would delete any other records owned by the old business unit.

Q. 47

1. Correct.
2. Incorrect. There is no Chart button on the Insert tab. To insert a chart, select the Sub-Grid button.
3. Correct.
4. Correct.
5. Incorrect. The chart type can only be changed by customizing the chart and cannot be changed in the List or Chart Properties window when inserting a chart into a form.

Q. 48

1. Incorrect. Security roles can only be used to grant or deny the task-based or entity-based security privileges.
2. Correct.
3. Incorrect. Database encryption is not a feature of Microsoft Dynamics CRM 2011.
4. Incorrect. The role-based forms do not restrict access to sensitive fields when using features such as Advanced Find.
5. Incorrect. The security privileges cannot be used to grant or deny access to fields.

Q. 49

1. Correct.
2. Correct.
3. Incorrect. The root parent business unit cannot be re-parented.
4. Incorrect. The root parent business unit cannot be deleted.
5. Incorrect. The root parent business unit cannot be deactivated.

Q. 50

1. Correct.
2. Incorrect. System views are available to all users and cannot be shared with or restricted to one team.
3. Incorrect. There is no such feature as a team view.
4. Incorrect. It is possible for a user to share his view with the custom team.
5. Incorrect. There is no feature to export a personal view.

Q. 51

1. Incorrect. There is no Copy View feature.
2. Incorrect. This method would include small, medium, and large accounts in the Large Customer Accounts view.
3. Incorrect. This method would create a view displaying accounts where the Customer Size is medium and small.
4. Incorrect. This method would create a view displaying accounts where the Customer Size is large, medium, and small.
5. Correct.

Q. 52

1. Incorrect. Only users with a System Administrator security role can import system charts.
2. Incorrect. This would make the chart available to all users in all business units.
3. Incorrect. There is no feature to limit system charts to users in the specified business units.
4. Correct.
5. Incorrect. It is possible to share a user chart.

Q. 53

1. Incorrect. All new solutions are unmanaged solutions.
2. Correct.
3. Correct.
4. Incorrect. You can export unmanaged solutions.
5. Incorrect. You can import managed solutions.

Q. 54

1. Incorrect. Lookup fields are not displayed by default on a new mobile form.
2. Correct.
3. Incorrect. Recommended fields are not displayed by default on a new mobile form.
4. Incorrect. Fields displayed on main forms are not displayed by default on a new mobile form.
5. Incorrect. Required fields are displayed by default on a new mobile form.

Q. 55

1. Incorrect. It is possible to meet this requirement without custom development.

2. Incorrect. The Claims Associated View filters are active records by default, so settled claims would not be displayed.

3. Correct.

4. Incorrect. An iFrame is not necessary.

5. Incorrect. Views cannot be added to a form.

Q. 56

1. Incorrect. No entities would be deleted.

2. Incorrect. No entities would be deleted.

3. Incorrect. No entities would be deleted.

4. Incorrect. No entities would be deleted.

5. Correct.

Q. 57

1. Incorrect. Solutions do not have a Can be customized property.

2. Incorrect. Only an unmanaged entity's Can be customized property can be modified.

3. Correct.

4. Incorrect. The entities in a managed solution cannot be customized.

5. Incorrect. Modifying the XML within a managed solution file is not supported.

Q. 58

1. Correct.

2. Incorrect. There is no Charts link in the main application screen.

3. Correct.

4. Correct.

5. Incorrect. Charts are visible to all users.

Q. 59

1. Incorrect. The standard chart types are column, bar, line, pie, and funnel charts.
2. Correct.
3. Incorrect. The standard chart types are column, bar, line, pie, and funnel charts.
4. Correct.
5. Correct.

Q. 60

1. Correct.
2. Incorrect. By default, only users with a System Administrator or System Customizer security role have access to custom forms.
3. Incorrect. Security role can also be used to control access to forms.
4. Incorrect. The field-security profiles are related to the field-level security feature and not to the role-based forms feature.
5. Correct.

Q. 61

1. Incorrect. Deployment-level auditing is not a feature of the CRM Deployment Manager.
2. Incorrect. Database-level auditing is not a feature of Microsoft Dynamics CRM 2011.
3. Correct.
4. Correct.
5. Correct.

Q. 62

1. Correct.
2. Incorrect. System and custom fields can be audited.
3. Incorrect. System and custom fields can be audited.
4. Incorrect. System and custom entities can be audited.
5. Incorrect. System and custom entities can be audited.

Q. 63

1. Incorrect. Audit records are not created when users run a report.
2. Incorrect. Audit records are not created when users run a query by using Advanced Find.
3. Correct.
4. Correct.
5. Incorrect. Users cannot delete audit records.

Q. 64

1. Incorrect. There is no feature to shrink an audit log.
2. Incorrect. There is no feature to export an audit log to file.
3. Incorrect. Only the oldest audit log can be deleted.
4. Correct.
5. Incorrect. There is no feature to export an audit log to file.

Q. 65

1. Incorrect. The Audit History View for a record cannot be viewed if the record has been deleted.
2. Correct.
3. Incorrect. Advanced Find cannot be used to query audit data.
4. Incorrect. The Filtered Views do not contain audit data.
5. Incorrect. The audit logs cannot be separated from the CRM database.

Q. 66

1. Incorrect. CRM would not be accessible if the database server storage is full.
2. Correct.
3. Incorrect. User access auditing is not required to audit the changes to records.
4. Correct.
5. Incorrect. Even if no fields are configured for auditing, audit records are still created for events such as when the record is created.

Q. 67

1. Incorrect. The default solution cannot be exported as a managed solution.
2. Incorrect. The default solution cannot be deleted.
3. Correct.
4. Incorrect. The display name of the default solution cannot be modified.
5. Correct.

Q. 68

1. Correct.
2. Incorrect. A publisher does not have to be a Microsoft partner and a Microsoft Partner Network membership number is not a field on the publisher record.
3. Correct.
4. Incorrect. Suffix is not a field on the publisher record.
5. Incorrect. **Version** is a field on the solution record.

Q. 69

1. Incorrect. Solution import failures are not reported to anyone.
2. Correct.
3. Incorrect. Solution import failures are logged regardless of whether tracing is enabled on the CRM server or not.
4. Incorrect. Solution import failures are logged.
5. Incorrect. Solution import failures are not displayed in the solution's configuration page.

Q. 70

1. Incorrect. Solution components have a **Can be customized** managed property but solutions do not.
2. Incorrect. Managed solutions cannot be exported.
3. Correct.
4. Incorrect. Entities referenced from a managed solution are not exported when an unmanaged solution is exported.
5. Incorrect. Solutions cannot be combined.

Q. 71

1. Incorrect. Business units cannot be included in an exported solution.
2. Correct.
3. Correct.
4. Incorrect. Teams cannot be included in an exported solution.
5. Incorrect. The auditing settings cannot be included in an exported solution.

Q. 72

1. Incorrect. If you remove the custom entity from solutin A, it will remain in solution B.
2. Correct.
3. Correct.
4. Incorrect. If you remove the custom entity from solution A, the custon entity records will not be affected.
5. Incorrect. If you delete solution A, the custom entity will be unaffected.

Q. 73

1. Incorrect. Managed solutions cannot be exported, but unmanaged solutions can be exported.
2. Correct.
3. Correct.
4. Incorrect. Customization conflicts, except for those in user interface components, are resolved in favor of the last solution to be imported regardless of whether it was a managed or unmanaged solution.
5. Incorrect. Solution components from managed and unmanaged solutions can be added to another unmanaged solution.

Q. 74

1. Correct.
2. Incorrect. There is no managed property to enable new fields to be created.
3. Incorrect. An entity's schema name cannot be modified.
4. Correct.
5. Incorrect. There is no managed property to enable an entity in a managed solution to be deleted.

Q. 75

1. Incorrect. Exporting a solution as a managed solution leaves behind the unmanaged solution.

2. Incorrect. Removing the custom entities from your solution will leave them in the default solution.

3. Correct.

4. Incorrect. System entities cannot be deleted.

5. Correct.

B
Answers to the Self-test Questions

In this section, you'll find the answers to the self-test questions from chapters 2 to 8.

Chapter 2: Configuring the System Settings

Question Number	Answers
1	2
2	1, 2 and 4
3	2 and 4
4	2
5	2

Chapter 3: Configuring the Organization Structure

Question Number	Answers
1	2
2	1 and 2
3	1 and 3
4	2
5	1, 4 and 5

Chapter 4: Entity and Attribute Customization

Question Number	Answers
1	2
2	2 and 5
3	1, 3 and 4
4	1 and 4
5	1 and 3

Chapter 5: Data Modelling Using Entity Relationships

Question Number	Answers
1	1, 2 and 5
2	4
3	3 and 5
4	3
5	2, 3, 4 and 5

Chapter 6: User Interface Customization: Forms, Views, and Charts

Question Number	Answers
1	1, 4, and 5
2	1 and 2
3	3
4	2, 3 and 4
5	1 and 3

Chapter 7: Auditing

Question Number	Answers
1	1
2	2 and 5
3	4

Chapter 8: Solutions

Question Number	Answers
1	1
2	2
3	4
4	4
5	4

C
Introduction to Microsoft Dynamics CRM Training and Certification

If you are new to the Microsoft Dynamics CRM training courses and certifications, the first half of this chapter will provide a useful overview of the official courses, exams, and certifications that are available. In the second half of the chapter, we'll learn how to book for the MB2-866 exam, what to expect, how to make best use of your time, and how to answer the exam questions.

In this chapter, we'll learn about Microsoft Dynamics CRM 2011:

- Training courses and examinations
- Certifications
- Exam MB2-866 — Customization and Configuration

Training courses and examinations

In this section, we'll learn about the official training courses and exams available for Microsoft Dynamics CRM 2011.

On the Microsoft Learning website (`http://learning.microsoft.com`), you can find more information about Mircosoft courses and exams. Here, you can also find a local training course provider or buy an online training course collection.

For users

Microsoft Dynamics CRM 2011 users will find the following two courses useful:

- **What's New in Microsoft Dynamics CRM 2011 (course 80289A)**: This one-day course provides an introduction to the new features of CRM 2011 to the users who already have experience with Microsoft Dynamics CRM 4.0.

- **Introduction to Microsoft Dynamics CRM 2011 (Course 80442A)**: This one-day course provides an overview of CRM 2011 to users with no previous experience with Microsoft Dynamics CRM.

There are no exams or certifications associated with these courses.

For implementers and administrators

If you are an implementation team member or a system administrator, there are eight training courses and four exams available.

Applications

There are four courses available for learning about the major application areas of Microsoft Dynamics CRM 2011:

- **Marketing Automation in Microsoft Dynamics CRM 2011 (Course 80290A)**: This one-day course covers the marketing features of CRM 2011. These marketing features include campaigns and quick campaigns, lists, templates, campaign activities, and campaign responses.

- **Sales Management in Microsoft Dynamics CRM 2011 (Course 80291A)**: This one-day course covers the sales features of CRM 2011. These sales features include leads, opportunities, quotes, orders, invoices, and the product catalog.

- **Service Management in Microsoft Dynamics CRM 2011 (Course 80292A)**: This one-day course covers the service management features of CRM 2011. These features include cases, queues, teams, and the knowledge base.

- **Service Scheduling in Microsoft Dynamics CRM 2011 (Course 80293A)**: This one-day course covers the service scheduling features of CRM 2011. These features include services, service activities, and the service calendar.

There is one exam covering all four of the application areas. This exam is **Microsoft Dynamics CRM 2011 Applications (Exam MB2-868)**. After passing this exam, you will earn a **Microsoft Dynamics Certified Technology Specialist (MCTS)** certification.

There are two other useful courses available for implementers and administrators. These courses are as follows:

- **Reporting in Microsoft Dynamics CRM 2011 (Course 80445A)**: This one-day course covers the advanced reporting features of CRM 2011. There is no exam associated with this course.

- **Workflow and Dialog Processes in Microsoft Dynamics CRM 2011 (Course 80444A)**: This one-day course covers the configuration and use of the workflows and dialogs processes in CRM 2011. There is no exam associated with this course.

There are no exams or certifications associated with these courses.

Installation

There is a training course and an exam that covers the installation and deployment of Microsoft Dynamics CRM 2011:

- **Microsoft Dynamics CRM 2011 Installation and Deployment (Course 80296A)**: This two-day course covers the deployment options, pre-requisites, and installation procedures for Microsoft Dynamics CRM 2011.

- **Microsoft Dynamics CRM 2011 Installation and Deployment (Exam MB2-867)**: After passing this exam, you will earn a MCTS certification.

Customization

There is a training course and an exam that covers the customization of Microsoft Dynamics CRM 2011:

- **Microsoft Dynamics CRM 2011 Customization and Configuration (Course 80294B)**: This three-day course covers the customization features of CRM 2011. These features include configuring the organization structure, customizing entities, forms, views, and charts.

- **Microsoft Dynamics CRM 2011 Customization and Configuration (Exam MB2-866)**: After passing this exam, you will earn a MCTS certification.

For developers

For developers there is one CRM 2011 training course and an exam available.

Extending

In addition to the Extending Microsoft Dynamics CRM 2011 training course and exam, developers should also consider the Microsoft Dynamics CRM 2011 Customization and Configuration training course and exam listed earlier in this chapter.

- **Extending Microsoft Dynamics CRM 2011 (Course 80295A)**: This three-day course covers the CRM 2011's extensibility options described in the Microsoft Dynamics CRM 2011 SDK.

- **Extending Microsoft Dynamics CRM 2011 (Exam MB2-876)**: After passing this exam, you will earn a MCTS certification.

Certifications

This section describes the two levels of certification available for Microsoft Dynamics CRM 2011 and the benefits of becoming certified.

Microsoft Certified Technology Specialist (MCTS)

MCTS certifications demonstrate your proficiency in a feature area of a Microsoft product. Passing any one of the four CRM 2011 exams described earlier in this chapter will earn you a MCTS certification.

Microsoft Certified IT Professional (MCITP)

MCITP certifications demonstrate your in-depth expertise across a number of Microsoft products. There are three MCITP certifications available:

- MCITP Applications for Microsoft Dynamics CRM
- MCITP Developer for Microsoft Dynamics CRM
- MCITP Installation and Configuration for Microsoft Dynamics CRM

At the time of writing, the MCITP certifications were still based on Microsoft Dynamics CRM 4.0 and Microsoft had not yet updated the MCITP certifications to include Microsoft Dynamics CRM 2011.

Benefits of certification

Whether you work for yourself as an independent consultant, or work for a Microsoft customer, or work for a Microsoft partner, earning a Microsoft Dynamics CRM certification leads the way to better career opportunities.

Microsoft partners value the certified individuals because employing Microsoft certified professionals enables them to achieve silver and gold competencies that demonstrate their commitment to, and expertise in, Microsoft Dynamics CRM.

Microsoft customers value the certified individuals because Microsoft Dynamics CRM solutions implemented, managed, and supported by the Microsoft-certified professionals have a lower total cost of ownership and a higher return on investment.

Achieving certification demonstrates the technical proficiency that validates your knowledge, adds credibility to your resume, and will help you advance in your career. When combined with real-world experience, certification will mean you are more highly regarded than other individuals with similar experience who haven't taken training or shown sufficient initiative to achieve certification.

Exam MB2-866—customization and configuration

The focus of this certification guide is exam MB2-866 — Microsoft Dynamics CRM 2011 Customization and Configuration. In this section we'll learn:

- How to study for the exam
- How to book your exam
- What to expect at the test center
- How to make best use of your time
- How to answer the different types of questions

How to study for the exam

There are several ways to study for the MB2-866 exam:

- **Take an official instructor-led training course**: *Course 80294B: Microsoft Dynamics CRM 2011 Customization and Configuration* is a three-day, instructor-led classroom training course available for a fee from Microsoft Learning Partners worldwide in a number of languages.

- **Take an official e-learning course**: A subscription to e-learning *Collection 80294: Customization and Configuration in Microsoft Dynamics CRM 2011* is available for a fee from Microsoft Learning in a number of languages.

- **Study the official courseware**: If your organization has purchased a Microsoft Dynamics service plan, you can download the official courseware for *Course 80294B: Microsoft Dynamics CRM 2011 Customization and Configuration* from PartnerSource or CustomerSource.

- **Use this certification guide**: This certification guide follows the syllabus examined in the MB2-866 Microsoft Dynamics CRM 2011 Customization and Configuration exam.

The best study method will depend upon your training budget, learning style, and the available time. This certification guide is the only option available that includes practice exam questions.

Hands-on experience

Hands-on experience with Microsoft Dynamics CRM 2011 is essential, regardless of your preferred study method. Follow all the procedures covered in this guide several times in a CRM test environment. Use a 30-day trial subscription to Microsoft Dynamics CRM Online, if you don't have a training deployment available. You don't need to have completed a full implementation project, but some hands-on experience will greatly improve your chances of success.

How to book your exam

Regardless of which study method you choose, the only way to book your MB2-866 exam is with Prometric—Microsoft's official certification exam provider.

Visit the Prometric website to book your exam (`http://www.prometric.com/Microsoft/Dynamics.htm`).

You must take your exam in-person at one of the Prometric's worldwide test centers. Candidates can use any test center, except in India, China, or Pakistan where you must provide proof that you are a legitimate resident of that country.

If you are taking an official training course with a Microsoft Learning Partner, check whether or not the course includes an exam before you book directly with Prometric.

Exam languages

MB2-866 is available in the following languages:

- Chinese (simplified)
- German
- English (American)
- Spanish (Castillian)
- French
- Italian
- Portuguese (Brazilian)
- Russian

Exam fees

The exam fees for MB2-866 are US$ 150 (at the time of writing). The exam fees in your country may vary.

Your organization may be entitled to, or have purchased, exam credits. Check with your manager before booking your exam.

Retaking the exam

If you need to retake your exam, you will need to rebook with Prometric and pay for your re-take exam. If you need to re-take the exam for a third time, you will need to wait 14 days after the date of your second exam.

What to expect at the test center

Prometric test centers are located in a wide variety of IT training and test centers worldwide. Microsoft Learning Partners often have a test center so that you can take the exam straight after completing an instructor-led training course.

You should arrive at the test center about 30 minutes before you are scheduled to take your exam. You will be asked to present a photographic identification to the test center administrator and to sign in to a log book.

You cannot take anything into the exam room with you. This certification guide is so exciting that it can be hard to put down, but you'll have to while taking your exam!

The exam room usually has a number of workstations screened off from each other and you may be taking your MB2-866 exam along with candidates taking the same or different exams. Communicating with other candidates is not allowed.

An exam supervisor will set up the exam on your computer and may or may not remain in the exam room during your exam. Video surveillance might be installed in the exam room to ensure all candidates comply with the exam rules.

A wipe-clean notepad will be provided, but any notes you take during the exam cannot be retained after the exam.

How to make best use of your time

Once the test center administrator has set up the exam on your computer, you will be able to start the exam. You have three hours to complete 75 exam questions, although some of this time will be spent reading the legal preamble regarding copyright and personal data protection.

Almost all candidates will comfortably complete the exam within the time limit. The questions in your test are taken at random from a large pool of possible questions, so no two exams will ever be exactly the same.

The passing marks are 700 points, but Prometric does not reveal the points awarded for each question.

Here are some tips to help you make the best use of your time:

- Spend lots of time in reading the terms and conditions, privacy statements, and other legal preamble only if you've missed your calling to the legal profession. Otherwise, accept the statements and move on to the exam as quickly as possible.

- Read each question carefully. In particular, pay attention to phrases that indicate how many answers are required—select one, choose three, or select all that apply—and whether you are expected to select true or false statements.

- Answer each question as best you can in sequence. Do not skip questions by leaving them unanswered. Instead, if you are not confident in your answer, mark the question for review at the end.

- After you have answered all the questions, reassess all the questions that you have marked for review.

- Before finishing the exam, quickly review all your answers to ensure you have left no questions unanswered, and where appropriate you have provided the required number of answers.

- Your intuition is often right. Change an answer only if you have an overwhelming feeling that your first answer was wrong.

How to answer the questions

There are two types of multiple choice questions in the exam:

- Multiple choice with one correct answer (radio buttons)
- Multiple choice with multiple possible answers (checkboxes)

Read the question carefully to see how many answers are required.

Consider the following example question:

1. You are the CRM system administrator at Contoso, responsible for managing Contoso's Microsoft Dynamics CRM 2011 system.

   You have been asked to create several new users. The users already exist in Contoso's Active Directory.

   Which of the following methods can be used to create new CRM users (select all that apply)?

   1. New User form
   2. Active Directory synchronization
   3. New Multiple Users wizard
   4. Data Import wizard using the Users template
   5. Clone User wizard

In this question, the first paragraph simply sets some context for the question and does not require special attention.

The second paragraph sets up the question scenario and contains important information that may determine which of the possible answers is valid. In this example, we are told that the users already exist in Contoso's Active Directory, which might influence how we answer the question.

The third paragraph poses the question itself and tells us how many of the possible answers are valid. In this example, we must select all the valid possibilities for creating new users.

Let's look at the potential answers:

1. New User form. This answer looks correct.

2. Active Directory synchronization. Active Directory synchronization is a new feature of CRM Online, when purchased through the Office 365, but it cannot be used to create new users in CRM 2011. This is an example of a plausible but incorrect possible answer.

3. New Multiple Users wizard. This answer looks correct.

4. Data Import wizard using the Users template. This answer looks plausible but isn't covered in the course syllabus. This is an example of a correct answer that you would only know if you had hands-on experience with CRM 2011.

5. Clone User wizard. There is no Clone User wizard so this answer looks incorrect. This is another example of a plausible but incorrect answer.

So the correct answer to this question is 1, 3, and 4.

Off-syllabus questions

This question is a good example of an off-syllabus question that sometimes appears in Microsoft certification exams. The Microsoft training course syllabuses and exams are written by different groups of people and do not always cover exactly the same material. So, it is possible to encounter an exam question that wasn't included in the syllabus.

This guide covers the course syllabus and a deep understanding of all the material covered here will be sufficient to achieve a passing score, but broader hands-on experience and additional reading is recommended, if you want to achieve a perfect score.

Summary

Microsoft offers a number of training courses, exams, and certifications for Microsoft Dynamics CRM 2011. The MB2-866 Microsoft Dynamics CRM 2011 Customization and Configuration exam is a multiple choice test with 75 questions to be answered in three hours. The recommended approach is to answer all the questions in sequence and mark any difficult questions for review at the end of the exam.

Index

Thank you for buying
Microsoft Dynamics CRM 2011 Customization & Configuration (MB2-866) Certification Guide

About Packt Publishing

Packt, pronounced 'packed', published its first book "Mastering phpMyAdmin for Effective MySQL Management" in April 2004 and subsequently continued to specialize in publishing highly focused books on specific technologies and solutions.

Our books and publications share the experiences of your fellow IT professionals in adapting and customizing today's systems, applications, and frameworks. Our solution based books give you the knowledge and power to customize the software and technologies you're using to get the job done. Packt books are more specific and less general than the IT books you have seen in the past. Our unique business model allows us to bring you more focused information, giving you more of what you need to know, and less of what you don't.

Packt is a modern, yet unique publishing company, which focuses on producing quality, cutting-edge books for communities of developers, administrators, and newbies alike. For more information, please visit our website: www.packtpub.com.

About Packt Enterprise

In 2010, Packt launched two new brands, Packt Enterprise and Packt Open Source, in order to continue its focus on specialization. This book is part of the Packt Enterprise brand, home to books published on enterprise software – software created by major vendors, including (but not limited to) IBM, Microsoft and Oracle, often for use in other corporations. Its titles will offer information relevant to a range of users of this software, including administrators, developers, architects, and end users.

Writing for Packt

We welcome all inquiries from people who are interested in authoring. Book proposals should be sent to author@packtpub.com. If your book idea is still at an early stage and you would like to discuss it first before writing a formal book proposal, contact us; one of our commissioning editors will get in touch with you.

We're not just looking for published authors; if you have strong technical skills but no writing experience, our experienced editors can help you develop a writing career, or simply get some additional reward for your expertise.

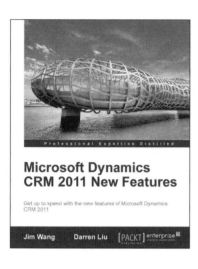

Microsoft Dynamics CRM 2011 New Features

Microsoft Dynamics CRM 2011 New Features

ISBN: 978-1-849682-06-0   Paperback: 288 pages

Get up to speed with the new features of Microsoft Dynamics CRM 2011

1. Master the new features of Microsoft Dynamics 2011

2. Use client-side programming to perform data validation, automation, and process enhancement

3. Work with the JRockit Mission Control 3.1/4.0 tools suite to debug or profile your Java applications

Microsoft Dynamics CRM 2011: Dashboards Cookbook

Microsoft Dynamics CRM 2011: Dashboards Cookbook

ISBN: 978-1-849684-40-8   Paperback: 266 pages

Over 50 simple but incredibly effective recipes for creating, customizing, and interacting with rich dashboards and charts

1. Take advantage of all of the latest Dynamics CRM dashboard features for visualizing your most important data at a glance.

2. Understand how iFrames, chart customizations, advanced WebResources and more can improve your dashboards in Dynamics CRM by using this book and eBook.

3. A highly practical cookbook bursting with a range of exciting task-based recipes for mastering Microsoft Dynamics CRM 2011 Dashboards.

Please check **www.PacktPub.com** for information on our titles

Microsoft Dynamics CRM 2011

Microsoft Dynamics CRM 2011 Application Design

ISBN: 978-1-849684-56-9   Paperback: 400 pages

Develop applications for any situation with our hands on guide to Microsoft Dynamics CRM 2011

1. Create your first application quickly and with no fuss

2. Develop in days what it has taken others years

3. Provide the solution to your company's problems

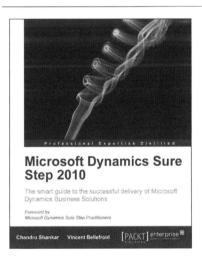

Microsoft Dynamics Sure Step 2010

ISBN: 978-1-849681-10-0   Paperback: 360 pages

The smart guide to the successful delivery of Microsoft Dynamics Business Solutions

1. Learn how to effectively use Microsoft Dynamics Sure Step to implement the right Dynamics business solution with quality, on-time and on-budget results.

2. Gain knowledge of the project and change management content provided in Microsoft Dynamics Sure Step.

3. Familiarize yourself with the approach to adopting the Microsoft Dynamics Sure Step methodology as your own.

Please check **www.PacktPub.com** for information on our titles

Made in the USA
San Bernardino, CA
16 June 2013